ALL TOGETHER NOW

VOL. 1

Professional Learning Communities and Leadership Preparation

Dr. Charles A. Guilford III

For more resources & information visit
theteacherteacherllc.com

Distributed by Bublish, Inc.

Paperback ISBN: 978-1-64704-203-5

"Thank you to my wife and son for their unwavering support and encouragement. I love you both immensely!!! To my family and friends, thank you for listening sharing, and keeping me sharp!!!"

Preface

When a problem is resolved, we tend to move on to the next one. Five-plus decades and the debate over educational reform processes still rages on, without a seemingly agreeable answer in view. Adding to the dilemma are the increasing efforts to resecure our schools. With all of this in mind, it raises the question "What now?" The following was birthed by twenty-plus years of educational experiences at various positions and levels and a cornucopia of educational research. There was no desire to add to the current backlog of quick fixes or cookie-cutter solutions that have plagued public education. Instead, the purpose was to find a means of improving public school performance that combines practitioner ownership, practical application, and relevant research. Whether or not the concept is embraced is beyond the control of the writer. However, the hope is that this text provides enough clarity of thought that decision-makers can add a viable option to their considerations. An option, by the way, supported by both practice and research. With that said, let us begin: All Together Now.

Dr. G (2019)

Introduction

K-12 education continues to underwhelm. Nationally, math and reading scores for the grades tested (fourth, eighth, and twelfth) continue to demonstrate an overall lack of proficiency.[1] The twelfth-grade scores are most alarming because (1) these students have had twelve years of schooling and (2) 84 percent of high school students are graduating, which suggests a gap between demonstrated abilities/skills and promotion. Academic achievement data is not the be-all and end-all, however, in the United States; though not suggested by researchers or educators, it is the means by which schools are measured.[2]

Even by these isolated measurement means, the American public school is underperforming, to put it mildly. Add in school violence, bullying, social inequality, sporadic workforce development, lack of resources, and low teacher efficiency and you have a pool of issues that remain unaddressed due to the lack of national, state, and local vision in regard to educating our students. The educational field, seemingly logically, depends on research to guide in the formulation of policy, procedure, curricula, and instructional practice.[3] How, then, does American public education remain unclear as to the direction in which to go?

Even with over seven decades of research on education, we do not have a foundation on which to build the best learning environments for our kids. It is not due to a lack of research. Reform proponents have championed school restructuring and process alteration for decades; however, the recommendations have fallen short of consensus.[4] The traditional structure of the American public education system has long been criticized for its antiquated and bureaucratic nature, which does not in any way foster the types of leadership recommended by research, or by practitioners, to improve student performance.[5] Forty years ago Ronald Edmonds (1979, 8) asserted that "(a) We can, whenever and wherever we choose, successfully teach all children whose schooling is of interest to us; (b) we already know more than we need to do that; and (c) whether or not we do it must finally depend on how we feel about the fact that we haven't so far." As Edmonds suggested, it is not that the needed information is not available, but there seems to be a lack of synthesis of available information. Basically, American public education is grocery shopping without knowing or using what is already in the fridge and cupboard. Thus, the field of public education remains in a constant state of perceived need. However, an examination and synthesis of prior and present research can shed some light on our current situation and, at the least, provide a feasible direction for improving American public schooling.

In regard to the best environments for improved student performance and educational leadership, past and present research suggest the following: (1) no one particular leadership approach/style/practice is sufficient within itself to dramatically impact or sustain all the necessary aspects of educational reform;[6] (2) quick fixes or one-size-fits-all approaches are insufficient for sustained educational reforms;[7] (3) the current responsibilities required of educational leaders are too much for one person to handle effectively;[8] (4) a localized, shared professional learning community, guided by a qualified central leadership figure, is most conducive to increased and sustainable positive student outcomes;[9] and (5) district policies must directly align with desired leadership practices.[10]

What do these trends suggest? They suggest that the ultimate goal of educational reform should be the building of professional learning communities (PLCs) within each school. The bureaucratic, top-down public-school structures have provided enough evidence of ineffectiveness. Localized, community-based schools operating under flexible district parameters are a possible solution. A clear understanding of what such an undertaking involves and how each respective stakeholder contributes is needed. *All Together Now: Vol. 1* focuses on the structural definitions, benefits, and training of leaders. Subsequent volumes will examine respective stakeholder responsibilities and preparation means. The information provided is a framework on which districts may structure their schools, while allowing for the flexibility of addressing specific regional and local needs. In addition, educational leader preparation programs can use the information to ensure that preparatory programs are aligned with district needs and expectations. While certain aspects are pertinent to fostering sustainable improvements, the framework is designed to allow for the flexibility that is recommended by decades of research.

PLC: The Public School's Ideal Structure

L ow-income / high-minority population, limited resources, urban. Typically, any combination of these adjectives would indicate a poor-performing school, even today. However, during the late '70s and early '80s performance abnormalities were occurring in urban schools with these traits.[11] So much so that numerous research endeavors were commissioned to determine the means by which these schools were defying outsiders' expectations.[12] While some research determined that these schools were performing highly as a result of specific concentrated "instructional" practices, others acknowledged, though in description alone, that the schools were actually functioning as professional learning communities.[13] Yes, the same schools that reportedly birthed the "instructional leadership model" were actually professional learning communities, based on the full identification and analysis of principals' practices.[14] An examination of multiple studies of these urban schools reveals that the schools were ultimately PLCs, as many of the relational aspects of the leaders' practices were omitted from the large body of research initially reported; it was also due to the fact that many of the schools, though desegregation had been outlawed, still operated in a segregated urban setting, which retained the community-based school environment common in minority schools prior to desegregation.[15] So what *are* professional learning communities, and what about them enables the progress of even the most unexpected segments of the public school population?

Professional learning communities are a form of shared leadership in which the administration, school staff, personnel, students, parents, and community members are engaged in reciprocal learning and leading.[16] More specifically, stakeholders are engaged in learning and leading that is aligned to meet the specific and localized needs of the students and reflects the values and beliefs of the community.[17] Brown (2016, 8) described the PLC as "team members who regularly collaborate toward continued improvement in meeting learner needs through a shared curricular-focused vision. Facilitating this effort are (1) supportive leadership and structural conditions; (2) collective challenging, questioning, and reflecting on team-designed lessons; and (3) instructional practices/experiences and team decisions on essential learning outcomes and intervention/enrichment activities based on results of common formative student assessments."

The need for professional learning communities is best described by Lambert's (2002, 5) statement: "We need to develop the leadership capacity of the whole school community. Out of that changed culture will arise a new vision of professional practice linking leading and learning." Fullan (2002, 4) cited the importance of the PLC by stating, "Creating and sharing knowledge is central to effective leadership. Information, of which we have a glut, only becomes knowledge through a social process. For this reason, relationships and professional learning communities are essential."

The distinction between the PLC and the general "shared leadership" construct is that the PLC ensures that all goals, tasks, procedures, and activities are directly aligned with the specific needs of the students in the building while also reflecting the values and interests of the school and community stakeholders for the purpose of improved instruction.[18]

In contrast, shared leadership predominantly focuses on ensuring consensus and task-load equity within an environment.[19] While shared leadership is the foundation of the PLC, its purpose is not as comprehensive. For example, Gautam, Alford, and Khanal (2015, 14) cited Hatch's (2013, 34) suggestion of "'instead of waiting for disruptive practices and technologies, we need to create the conditions for individuals, groups, and organizations to adapt, innovate, and improve all the time.'" Shared leadership would not specifically, in its basic form, support these types of conditions. More specific elements are needed, as Reed and Swaminathan (2014, 6) asserted: "The central tenets of PLCs include the following: collaborative cultures, the dismantling of teacher isolation, and highly effective teams that focus on learning." The PLC environment appears to supersede the demographic contexts that normally hinder full-on acceptance of culture-building approaches.[20] All stakeholders could benefit from the creation, implementation, and sustaining of PLC school cultures. In order to highlight the building culture improvements the PLC can provide, an examination of the benefits for key building stakeholders is provided.

Administrative Benefits

Leadership is vital to the effectiveness of the creation and sustaining of the PLC and requires a different work approach by building leaders. While the initial groundwork may seem daunting, the school administration benefits from the staff capacity building, improved school building culture, and feasible workload.

Staff Capacity Building

The changing administrative role, with increased responsibility and accountability, has led to the stark conclusion that the "hero model" of school leadership no longer suffices.[21] The PLC fosters principals' need to establish and build communities of leaders, which helps to remove the need for a "hero" leader.[22] Administrators that foster PLCs benefit from a school culture that enables staff capacity building by setting a focus for staff self-evaluation, learning, and improvement.[23]

Having a shared building vision, and aligning all activities and practices with it, enables the staff "to be nurtured and supported to develop skills and practices necessary to serve the diversity of student needs, to support and enhance performance of teachers, and engage multiple sectors of the community in the mission of achieving optimal outcomes for all students" (Masumoto, Brown-Welty 2009, 15). The staff focusing on instructional practices and "working, teaching, and helping one another" enables the administration to focus on the "big picture" of school improvement and not get bogged down by mundane tasks (Mendels 2012, 3). At the same time, the administration is increasing the expertise of staff to be utilized in future leadership capacities. The administrator serves, in the PLC, as the master educator who facilitates the leading and learning growth of staff.[24] This type of capacity building also assists with culture changing.

Improved School Building Culture

The school building culture can be the life or death of a school. The efficacy, beliefs, values, pride, and motivations of a building's staff have been noted as factors that can impact student achievement.[25] Administrators have a significant impact on building culture. Hallinger (2003, 2) asserted that "[the] evolution of the educational leadership role [. . .] is aimed primarily at changing the organization's normative structure." This includes the sharing of leadership, and with the staff's capacity increased, the principal can more readily perform the practices that increase the building's positive culture.[26]

The PLC structure allows administration the freedom to build and foster trusting and collaborative learning and leading cultures after they take the steps of capacity building. Capacity building relays the belief in the individual abilities and expertise of staff.[27] The building leader who fortifies a positive school culture can benefit greatly from the shared purpose and collaboration of the staff, students, parents, and community. A positive school culture allows for open interaction between administration and staff, staff and students, staff and parents, and all the other variations of interaction between local school stakeholders.[28] "Hero model" leaders are limited in their ability to sustain making time for fruitful and positive stakeholder interactions without sacrificing other important aspects of building leadership. The establishment of this culture is not simplistic; however, the benefits of the PLC far outweigh the burden of implementation. Also, a portion of the process would have already been done through the building of the staff's capacity. Both aforementioned benefits are worthwhile to improve a school's performance, but the last administrative benefit, discussed below, may address the taboo desire of many administrators.

Feasible Workload

The staff's ability to self-evaluate and improve, with guidance and support from administration combined with a more positive building culture, can lighten the workload of administrators. One of the biggest burdens of many schools, especially underperforming schools, is the hiring of highly qualified teachers.[29] Having high-quality staff that can share in the various instructional, and some managerial, tasks of a building increases the feasibility of the leader's workload.[30] The lightening of this burden alone would be the answer to many administrators' prayers. While the PLC does not eliminate the hiring of unqualified teachers, the collaborative, peer-to-peer building of skills assists with the burden, and the shared vision and beliefs serve as an organic deterrent for those unwilling to grow their skills to remain in the building.[31]

The various responsibilities of an administrator or administration can be overwhelming, and the need, especially today, for competent support is obvious. This competent support arises from a staff's opportunities to grow, improve, and lead, and the PLC culture fosters this organically.[32]

While the PLC supports and benefits administration, it is a shared environment. The sharing of the responsibility also fosters the sharing of the benefits for staff, students, and parents.

Staff Benefits

Sharing leadership can be ill-received by staff and viewed as "dumping" when followers are not viewed as partners, or are not sharing in the benefits. Currently, the implementation of shared leadership is being done without the policy and cultural requirements needed for sustainability. As a result, administrators are being encouraged to delegate tasks and seek stakeholder input; however, blame or praise still rests in the lap of the administration. This fragmented approach is the type of "dumping" that research warns of in regard to shared leadership.[33] The professional learning community culture provides not only the environment of partnership but also the benefits of improved staff efficacy, increased support, and better use of resources. Job satisfaction, lack of administrative support, and lack of resources top the list of reasons for teachers' dissatisfaction with the profession.[34] The benefits of the PLC described below focus solely on these concerns, as addressing these concerns would set the foundation for future improvements.

Improved Efficacy

Job satisfaction and efficacy have been directly linked to leadership in various research.[35] The building of teachers' efficacy begins with professional development and mastery experiences.[36] A school environment that fosters the identification of effective research/evidence-based strategies, in-service training, and student success likely increases teachers' willingness to try new approaches.[37] Purposeful professional development and mastery experiences provide a doubly beneficial belief that the teacher can impact and the student can be impacted. This belief is empowering, and teachers are more likely to engage in the implementation of new instructional practices when "their principal values them as a partner in the school program, and not just as a staff member" (Allen, Grigsby, and Peters 2015, 16). The PLC fosters the collaborative environment values needed to get its members to, as Ross and Gray (2006, 5) stated, "adopt instructional practices recommended by the [local] organization, assist colleagues, and work harder to achieve organizational goals." Improved staff support is another factor that can contribute to the teachers' efficacy and is an organic aspect of the PLC culture.

Improved Staff Support

Lack of administrative support is one of the top reasons a teacher stays at or leaves a school, and it has proven to impact teacher retention at respective school levels.[38] Much of the desired support pertains to basic management tasks (lesson planning, classroom management, parent interactions, etc.).[39] The current school structures and cultures place so much responsibility on the shoulders of administration that providing teachers with the types of support desired, and needed, is sporadic at best.[40] The desired supports require processes that, even in ideal settings, would be difficult for administration, by themselves, to sustain. The PLC culture can assist with alleviating some, if not most, of this burden. The PLC fosters an environment that is collective, collaborative, and supportive, which makes the supporting of staff a schoolwide responsibility, not just an administrative one.[41]

The PLC is founded on the reciprocal learning and leading of the staff, which can provide the type of basic supports desired by staff.[42]This type of unified support can provide teachers with a sense of trust and involvement that fosters increased purpose. Furthermore, since all supports, tasks, and procedures are aligned with the shared vision, not only are the basic support needs of the staff addressed, but more in-depth capacity building is fostered.[43] A staff that feels involved and supported can have greater impacts on student achievement.[44]

The PLC does not discourage administration from providing support for staff. On the contrary, it places leaders in the position of "master teachers" and allows them to enable the staff's self-improvement.[45] Simultaneously, it allows leaders to focus staff support efforts on individualized support for struggling staff. By fostering the ideal, collaborative school culture, staff members not only benefit from increased capacity and levels of support but also are more likely to get the types of resources they need.

Resources

The current school structures often function under a top-down directive flow (though selective autonomy has been granted in some districts). District-level administration determines curricular focuses and needed supplies and, though not always equitably, provides individual schools with the prescribed resources or means of obtaining them. The problem with this approach is that it overlooks the individual building's needs.[46] The resources are provided to move students to where the district believes they should be; however, rarely are resources provided to get students to the minimum threshold needed to meet the district's goals.

The concern is similar to the complaints of districts when the No Child Left Behind Act (NCLB) set goals but did not supply the needed resources and provisions to ensure an equal starting point. The by-product of overlooking local school needs is that building leaders are held accountable by staff when the resources are limited and/or do not meet the needs of the students they are charged with teaching. Lack of resources, another top reason for teacher attrition, does not necessarily imply that schools do not have supplies and materials. Instead, I will refer to resources as supplies and materials *that meet the specific needs of students in individual schools.* The PLC culture places a specific focus on aligning all aspects of building operations on the shared vision, including resources.[47] The current top-down structures do not allow for this type of alignment, because the resources supplied by the district are aligned with the district's vision, not the schools' specific needs.[48] The district's vision may encompass portions of the school-based vision, but because of the varied student populations, individualized student needs, and varied community cultures and values, it is highly unlikely that it specifically aligns with it.[49]

Ironically, a district's enveloping vision of growth for all is better served by granting autonomy to individual buildings in regard to curriculum and resources. The PLC culture fosters the leader's ability to ensure that the staff has all it needs to meet the needs of its students. If staff is not enabled with the tools needed to perform the tasks they have been trained and supported on, the trust and commitment garnered through the building of capacity and increased support can be undermined. The shared vision sets the foundation for the school's purpose, professional development is aligned, support is given, and then resources are provided. Without the last step, many teachers could deem the prior steps to be pointless. The PLC benefit of allowing schools to acquire and manipulate the resources specific to their shared school vision can assuage teachers' concerns about not having the needed tools to improve student performance.[50] This autonomous, in-building, and equitable resource acquisition and distribution strengthens the likelihood of teachers having mastery experiences, which contribute to efficacy and greater commitment.[51] In addition, the benefits that staff experience in the PLC can lead to benefits for students as well.

Student Benefits

The benefits of the PLC for students largely revolve around students' academic achievement, because of the limited availability of nonacademic school success evaluative tools.[52] Students in the PLC environment can benefit from increased academic performance and having an active voice in their educational process, which can lead to additional benefits.

Increased Achievement

Students' academic performance in PLC cultures is varied but largely positive. Aitkens (2009, 2) noted that "findings in the research strongly suggest that a participatory, collaborative model of leading and improving is the most effective way to learning improvement." Ross and Gray (2006, 15) also affirmed that "the strongest impact on achievement occurred through teacher commitment to school–community partnerships." The measurement of school success using only academic gains, which is the national norm, has been criticized as limited and antiquated.[53]

However, even by these means, traditional school structures, nationally, have struggled to meet even basic proficiency standards, as noted earlier. Higher levels of student achievement have resulted from collaborative, school-based–focused schools. The students in the PLC benefit from (1) a shared vision with students' needs as a priority, (2) development of teachers' capacity, (3) increased teacher efficacy and commitment, (4) alignment of resources to the shared vision, and (5) school autonomy to make school-based decisions that support the shared vision.[54] All of these elements have been noted as having significant impacts on students' academic achievement. The PLC also fosters a culture that encourages and incorporates students' voices in regard to their education.

Student Voice

Students, traditionally, have little input when it comes to what they are taught. The norm is that curriculum and skill focuses are determined outside of the school building, and students just show up and receive the prescribed lesson. At most, students may sporadically be granted permission to make activity suggestions for a specific lesson plan, but rarely in regard to what they will learn. In recent years, more "student-based" learning has been encouraged, but this is largely focused on students leading the prescribed lesson, not determining the means, ways, or content. However, in the professional learning community, student input is twofold: (1) visions and subsequent curriculum and practices are aligned to meet the specific needs of students, and (2) students have an active voice in their education.[55] The PLC, as mentioned previously, is focused on addressing the specific needs of the school's students. This specificity in alignment places the needs and interests of students at the forefront of all its actions, and thus, students organically provide input for the functioning of their educational experience.

In addition, the shared leadership construct provides all stakeholders with a voice in regard to the school's operations, students included. Students are given the opportunity to provide feedback, suggestions, and openly make requests based on their interests. Variation in perspective is vital to an organization's progression. Empowering students by providing them with a legitimate voice in regard to their education fosters a sense of ownership and belief in the school's purpose.[56] This empowerment of students' voices can lead to other benefits as well.

Additional Benefits

Education is more than academics. A school is more than a building. A leader is more than a person in charge. A teacher is more than a presenter. A student is more than grades. The PLC culture acknowledges these distinctions and fosters higher expectations than mere attainment of grades and test scores.[57] Unfortunately, national experts, policymakers, and others have yet to validate alternative means of evaluating school success.[58] This lack of validation does not discredit the fact that students can benefit in multiple ways from positive, collaborative, school-based learning communities. Day, Gu, and Sammons (2016, 3) articulated the need for alternative evaluation means and the alternative benefits successful learning environments can have for students:

> Although it is acknowledged that measurable outcomes of students' academic progress and achievement are key indicators in identifying school "effectiveness," they are insufficient to define "successful" schools. A range of leadership research conducted in many contexts over the past two decades shows clearly that "successful" schools strive to educate their pupils by promoting positive values (integrity, compassion, fairness, and love of lifelong learning), as well as fostering citizenship and personal, economic, and social capabilities. (Day and Leithwood 2007; Ishimaru 2013; Mulford and Silins 2011; Putnam 2002)

The PLC fosters the aforementioned benefits, and while all of these benefits may not yet be recognized as measurements of success, the implementation of PLC cultures can support the subsequent policy alignment of evaluation tools that do take these benefits into consideration. Since the PLC structure fosters the involvement of all stakeholders, parents/guardians reap the benefits as well.

Guardian Benefits

Student guardians are not exempt from the benefits of the establishment of professional learning communities. Parents/guardians have long been sought after as viable contributors to the educational process; however, their involvement has usually been dictated and limited. With the PLC implementation, guardians stand to benefit from having increased belief in the school's purpose, having an active voice, and having an increased ability to hold schools accountable.

Belief in the School's Purpose

The greatest benefit for guardians is the improved performance of their students. When collaborative, interactive, aligned, and reciprocal leading and learning school cultures are established, students perform better. The increase in student performance is not coincidental; it is a result of a culture that makes students' improvement its top priority.[59] Guardians are often critical of schools when their student does not perform well, largely because the ambiguity of the school's purpose leaves schools vulnerable to such criticism.[60] However, by implementing the PLC culture, the school makes its purpose and processes clear to all stakeholders, which impacts student performance and increases guardians' confidence in the school.

Parental confidence and belief impacts the interactions between guardians and the school's administration and staff.[61] A guardian's belief that the school has set their student's growth as its priority can decrease their inclination to view the school as an adversary and encourage them to view it more as a partner. The PLC culture also provides the guardian stakeholder with an active voice in the school.

Voice

The importance of having a voice in regard to your child's/ student's education cannot be understated. Guardians, like students, are usually just receptacles for the ideas, purposes, and practices of schools because rarely do they get to have input on what the school does instructionally. Yes, parent associations have been around for decades, but because districts usually determine instructional activities, guardians still tend to be bystanders for top-down initiatives. By creating school cultures that are shared and focused on all stakeholders' development in regard to leading and learning, guardians are given not only the opportunity to have a voice but also the knowledge and skills to effectively use their voice.[62] Guardians having an active voice can lead to more parent-initiated involvement, which is more impactful than the passive guardian participation fostered by the current school structures.[63] This voice contributes to guardians' sense of ownership of their student's learning and places them in a position to not only support the school's purposes but share in school accountability.

Increased Accountability

District leaders are largely responsible for the instructional focuses and practices that local schools implement; however, due to the limited local accessibility of district leaders, guardians are usually left with holding teachers and administrators accountable. This approach would work if the teachers and administrators had the autonomy to make suggested changes, but largely they do not.[64] Guardians, in turn, often perceive the inaction on the part of the building leaders as a passing of the buck and may not perceive administration as leaders. In the PLC, the guardian is a local stakeholder and thus has an active voice in the school.

Since the guardians are involved in and aware of the purposes and practices occurring in the building, and the leaders of the building have the autonomy to make needed changes, a greater level of accountability is placed in the hands of guardians. The PLC ensures that they do not have to wait for district board meetings or for the bureaucratic processes to play out. Guardians can be directly involved in decision-making and have a direct line to the other decision makers.[65]

The various local stakeholders stand to benefit greatly from a restructuring of the public school system. The localization of decision-making and instructional focuses provides the opportunity for greater ownership, participation, and improvement for school stakeholders, all with the intent of increasing student achievement. All of these benefits can be attained in the PLC school culture. Sporadic and fragmented infusion of shared leadership does not suffice in building and maintaining professional learning communities. An intentional, calculated, yet flexible process is needed to ensure PLC sustainability. This process hinges on the development of leadership. It is imperative that qualified central leadership figures be at the helm of PLC school environments in order to create, implement, and sustain them. Prerequisites for developing such leaders are defining educational leadership, examining the present and intended roles, and determining the skills needed to perform said roles.

Defining Leadership

With the target set on developing the best learning environments within our schools (the PLC), a few questions remain: (1) Who can facilitate these ideal learning communities; (2) how do we define the role of these facilitators; (3) what kind of skills and/or practices will these facilitators require; and (4) how do we enable these facilitators' success?

The researching and defining of the leadership construct continues to be an elusive task, one that has been going on for decades. There are as many definitions and perspectives as there is research pertaining to the topic. Bass (1990, 3) believed that "superior leadership performance [. . .] occurs when leaders broaden and elevate the interests of their employees when they generate awareness and acceptance of the purposes and mission of the group, and when they stir their employees to look beyond their own self-interest for the good of the group." Carraway (1990, 10) proposed that "in essence, leadership is a relationship between the leader and the follower. It cannot exist by itself; it exists only if followship is produced." Krug (1990, 8) argued that "effective leaders provide the organization with a combination of technical skills and 'functional' skills." As more research was conducted, more variances on the concept of leadership developed. Portin (1997, 5), in citing Foster (1989, 49), noted that "Foster, in writing from the perspective of critical theory, reminds leadership theorists and practitioners that 'leadership, then, is not a function of position but rather represents a conjunction of ideas where leadership is shared and transferred between leaders and followers, each only a temporary designation.'" Current research has provided minimal clarity on the leadership topic. If the definition of the general concept of leadership continues to be evasive and varied, then the definition of the educational leader is no different.

The practices, training, and role of educational leaders have been scrutinized, altered, and debated for at least the past fifty years.[66] This research pool has provided the foundation for many of the recent (2000s–present) studies, articles, and analyses. Recent research information on the topic of educational leadership has resulted in few, if any, new practitioner approaches or understanding.[67] Largely, it has resulted in more rehashing, rebranding, and minuscule alterations to information established by the prior fifty years of research. Moreover, it has led to a continued debate as to the best model for increasing student achievement, namely, transformational or instructional leadership.[68] The inconsistency in defining the educational leader construct could be largely due to the continually changing role of the educational leader.

Educational Leader Role Change

Headmaster, principal, master teacher—all of these titles have been or are terms used for the person in charge of a school. Just as the titles have changed, the role of the head of a school has changed as well. Portin (1997, 3) identified the educational reform environment as a key factor in the role fluctuation by stating, "The pressures for school reform, legislated reform initiatives, and school restructuring are fundamentally affecting principals. School-based decision making, deregulated state structures, increased social complexity, curriculum reforms, and a host of other changes have altered principals' roles." Luu (2010, 1) eloquently described the role transition by stating the following:

> The role of the principal has changed dramatically in the last few decades. It used to be a role that involved a paternalistic school leader who managed staff, students, and operations with a firm hand.

> The role of principal has since evolved into one in which the principal must understand the needs of their students, staff, community and the curriculum.

It is clear that the role of the school leader is ever-changing and increasingly demanding. Also, the fact remains that no single leadership model suffices in preparing school leaders to moderately sustain current improvement expectations, let alone create, implement, and sustain a PLC.[69] The ever-changing role and/or push for shared leadership does not remove or diminish the need for a qualified, central leadership figure in a school building. Research has made it clear that a "captain," not a "hero," is needed in all school buildings.

Need for a Qualified Central
Leadership Figure

No matter the desired school environment, a qualified central leadership figure is needed.[70] The recent push for shared/distributed leadership often understates the importance of a central figure. The shared approach is sometimes championed as a democratic utopia devoid of a "leader" and guided by the collective leadership of the whole. Ironically, in order to create, implement, and sustain a shared leadership environment, a qualified central leadership figure is imperative.[71] This is even more true in regard to the PLC. Leech and Fulton (2008, 5) succinctly stated that "the importance of the role of the principal as change agent and instructional leader consistently appears in the research on change and effective schools."

Shouppe and Pate (2010, 2) explained the need for the central figure by stating, "A number of studies dating back to the 1970s have investigated characteristics of effective schools (e.g., Edmonds 1979; Fullan 1993; Good and Brophy 1986; Lezotte 1991), and much has been reported on specific correlates, including the need for strong leadership." Similar to most team constructs, a "coach" is needed to ensure that all the respective members stay focused on the shared vision, which, in turn, allows the followers to focus on their respective tasks. In the shared leadership construct, the goal is to empower the content experts for the good of the students. Their expertise is honed to contribute to the school's vision. The shared construct is not intended to eliminate the need for a principal, but rather to empower and enable staff to use their abilities to the utmost.[72]

The PLC takes the shared construct to an even higher level. In the PLC, not only is leadership shared but the development of staff, goals, and practices are all aligned for the building's purposes.[73] For example, instead of the English department solely focusing on the English curriculum, they reciprocally engage, share practices, observe, critique, and professionally develop with other departments in order to meet the shared vision. In this case, the central figure is needed to ensure that these cross-curricular engagements occur and to provide any needed supports and/or resources.[74] But in order to create, implement, and sustain a professional learning environment, there are certain skills an educational leader will need in order to be considered qualified. Based on the magnitude of research available, it is believed that by identifying the ideal school culture (PLCs) and the type of practices/skills a leader needs to fortify said culture, a clearer definition of an educational leader may emerge, thus improving the preparation processes of educational leadership, which will ultimately lead to increased student achievement.

Qualified Central Leadership Figure Skill Set Needs

The PLC environment requires a cultural shift away from the traditional bureaucratic school structures. Even if shared leadership has been implemented, an additional shift to greater responsibilities and productivity is required. A principal would need to transform their staff and building. In order to orchestrate this type of transformation, the leader of the building would need a clear grasp of the transformational framework and the supportive instructional, shared, and professional learning community focuses.[75]

Transformational Framework

Burns defined transformational leadership as "a process where leaders and followers engage in a mutual process of raising one another to higher levels of morality and motivation" (Northouse 2013, 187). According to Burns, "the transforming approach creates significant change in the life of people and organizations" (Northouse 2013, 189). Burns argued that "through training, managers can learn the techniques and obtain the qualities they need to become transformational leaders" (Bass 1990, 19). This concept was fleshed out even further when Bass (1985, 7) said that transformational leaders focus on motivating, intellectual stimulation, and individual considerations. Bass identified specific behaviors that transformational leaders displayed in order to transform organizations: Idealized Influence, Inspirational Motivation, Intellectual Stimulation, and Individualized Consideration.[76] Kouzes and Posner (2007, 122, 15) furthered the concept of transformational leadership practices in their book *The Leadership Challenge* by stating, "Transformational leadership is the kind of leadership that gets people to infuse their energy into strategies." These researchers identified five practices of exemplary leaders: (1) Model the Way, (2) Inspire a Shared Vision, (3) Challenge the Process, (4) Enable Others to Act, and (5) Encourage the Heart. These practices are directly aligned with Bass's initial interpretation of transformational leadership.

Pugh et al. (2011, 1) described the relationship between the Five Leadership Practices (transformational leadership) and education by stating, "Effective leadership for 21st Century schools depends, to a great extent, on the principal's ability to inspire, enable, and motivate faculty while concurrently modeling professional behaviors and challenging the status quo." Many studies have been conducted that demonstrate a correlation between transformational leadership and student achievement.

Educational leaders who exhibit the key traits of transformational leadership are positively related to better employee performance. In a study by Natalia Campbell, EdD, of the Wadsworth Magnet School for High Achievers, findings revealed that "transformational leadership of the school administration team paved the way for success" (Campbell 2013, 203). Balyer (2012, 3, 5–11) used the qualitative study approach to examine the major characteristics of transformational leadership among principals and their impact on schools. This study revealed that principals who demonstrated idealized influence, inspirational motivation, individualized consideration, and intellectual stimulation, all of which are the major components of transformational leadership, had increased school performance and teacher satisfaction. Nash's (2010, 56–57) study explored the use of transformational leadership practices among students who are generally considered at-risk. The study examined principals' leadership styles among "poor, black, brown and linguistically diverse students." Nash concluded that "transformational leadership existed among principals in the sample, [and] it was significantly correlated with students' achievement in certain areas." Ross and Gray (2006, 812) concluded that "principals who adopt a transformational leadership style are likely to have a positive impact on teacher beliefs about their collective capacity and on teacher commitment to organizational values." Subsequently, the impact on the teachers is believed to lead to an indirect and modest impact on student achievement. The impact of transformational leadership in schools has been solidified through multiple research efforts.[77] However, there is a specific reason that this research refers to transformational leadership as a framework and not a model.

The adoption, and subsequent implementation, of transformational leadership as the leading form of educational leader training, operation, and evaluation was a result of research findings within the political and business communities.[78] Educational leaders, researchers, and policymakers deemed this newfound approach a desirable model for increasing principals' effectiveness in improving school productivity and, subsequently, student achievement. The educational field deemed this approach worthwhile, since the results of the leaders in other fields who demonstrated these transformational approaches were undeniable. While the data and information gleaned from the generic leadership practices' research were promising, proponents of this model for use in the educational field overlooked or did not account for a key aspect: the need for contextual adjustment of the practices described as transformational.[79]

When examining the original implementation of the transformational leadership approach in the educational setting, leaders' approaches downplayed the essential functioning of a school, which is instruction. Instead, the leaders' practices were geared toward prescribed, generalized leadership practices focused on "humanistic facilitators" and encouraging compliance (Lashway 2003, 3). While the transformational leaders were thought to be moving the schools toward greater efficiency and achievement, it was determined, through research and data, that the impacts were not as great as expected.[80] Over time, it was clear that these transformational leaders were not equipped with the contextual and pedagogical knowledge needed to effectively transform the schools as anticipated. The fault was not in the leaders' application of the prescribed and generic transformational leadership practices or behaviors; the fault was in the lack of contextual adjustment of said practices and behaviors.

It was progressive for educational leaders, researchers, and policymakers to recognize the impacts of the transformational leadership style. Even so, as has been the modus operandi, they assumed that transformational leadership could simply be transferred into the educational setting without any adjustments—the "cookbook" approach.[81] The misinterpretation of transformational leadership, though not solely the educators' fault, was the belief that transformational leadership itself was *how* leaders lead. In actuality, transformational leadership is a frame construct that indicates *what* leaders should do: transform their organizations. The transformational construct initially focused on two areas: (1) initializing and organizing work, and (2) showing consideration for employees (Bass 1990, 21).

The implementation error on the part of educators was not recognizing that the suggested practices were derived from a for-profit setting and therefore focused the leader's practices/behaviors on the kind of initializing and organizing that was beneficial to a for-profit setting. While educators may have believed this corporate model would add to the efficiency of the educational structure, the lack of attention paid to the leaders' acquisition and understanding of pedagogical knowledge and awareness of the nonprofit, bureaucratic structure of school contexts proved problematic. Ironically, even with this erroneous application of the transformational model, impacts were still made, though not to the anticipated levels. These impacts suggest the power of the transformational framework for use by educational leaders.

Transformational leadership is used as a framework, not a model, for the purposes of this synthesis. By interpreting transformational leadership as a framework, the limitations of replicating the business model practices are removed, and thus effective contextual manipulation of the framework is permitted. The five practices of exemplary leaders, developed by Kouzes and Posner, is the most effective transformational framework to use, as it efficiently consolidates the practice focuses needed to transform any organization. However, transformational leadership in isolation has less impact than instructionally focused practices because its generic form does not meet the contextual needs of the educational environment. Therefore, in order for an educational leader to possess the skills to implement the PLC culture, additional skill focuses are needed.

Instructional Focus

As noted earlier, in urban schools a phenomenon had occurred. Poor black youth were performing academically at unexpected levels. The aberration was not ignored. Multiple research studies were conducted to determine the means by which the principals of these schools were achieving success.[82] The findings from the "effective schools movement" was "the identification of instructional leadership as a significant aspect of effective schools" (Mendez-Morse 1992, 17). Once identified, instructional leadership was cited as more impactful and conducive to the educational setting than transformational, and thus the new model was pushed as the ideal educational leadership approach.

Examination of the research on these aberrational schools revealed that the principals actually fostered professional learning communities.[83] Since a PLC is a higher form of shared leadership, obviously these principals would have needed to establish shared leadership first. Research by Printy, Marks and Bowers (2010, 3) noted that "transformational leadership by the principal appears to be a necessary but insufficient condition for activating shared instructional leadership." This note, combined with a detailed analysis and categorization of the practices performed by the researched principals (especially those omitted by many popular studies), reveal that the principals in these urban schools were actually transformational.[84]

It appears, based on their described behaviors, that these principals had already adjusted transformational leadership for the educational context. Niece (1989), as cited by Mendez-Morse (1992, 38), noted that the principals of some of these urban schools "had identified eight additional dimensions of instructional leadership not listed by experts, six of which targeted people or interpersonal abilities." In addition, Krug (1990, 10) cited Murphy's (1988) criticism of the instructional leadership model:

> In his review of assessment problems facing the area of instructional leadership, Murphy (1988) outlined three major problems; (a) atheoretic, descriptive approaches that downplay the importance of explanatory models, (b) focusing on too limited a range of easily observable behaviors, and (c) ignoring stylistic or personal factors that help define the seven set[s] of behaviors effective administrators use.

This distinction is vital because the omission of some of the studied principals' key practices allowed for the erroneous identification of a "new" leadership model: instructional. In actuality, these progressive principals embodied the idea that transformational leadership was a framework needing to be adjusted for the context of the educational field.

The misidentification of "instructional leadership" is why, for the purposes of this text, it is referred to as an instructional focus within the transformational framework.

It is only recently that researchers have suggested that "integrated" models (combining transformational and instructional practices) would be the best leadership approach.[85] The integrated model suggests the combining of two separate constructs, when in reality there appears to be one framework (transformational) that allows for multiple leadership focuses.[86] It is vital that this distinction be made, because the debate of transformational versus instructional leadership appears to have stagnated the progression of the educational leader due to research focusing studies on these two topics as separate leadership types.[87] This distinction can change the viewpoint of leadership constructs, practice acquisition, and research.

The instructional focus serves to show "how" educational leaders lead; leaders will use instructionally focused practices to transform their schools into PLCs. Most recently, principals have been viewed as needing to be focused on instruction and not management. Leithwood et al. (2004, 5) asserted in their research that "leadership is second only to classroom instruction as an influence on student learning." Further research helped to identify school characteristics that typified the success of instructionally focused leaders, which include a learning climate free of disruption, a system of clear teaching objectives, and high teacher expectations for students (Bossert, Dwyer, Rowan, and Lee 1982). Bossert et al. (1982, 35) further asserted that these school characteristics are fostered by principals that "provide coherence to their schools' instructional programs, conceptualize instructional goals, set high academic standards, stay informed of policies and teachers' problems, make frequent classroom visits, create incentives for learning, and maintain student discipline." Robinson, Lloyd and Rowe (2008, 640) found that instructionally focused leadership had a three to four times greater impact on student achievement than transformational leadership alone.

Although data have supported the positive impact of instructionally focused leadership, there are contrasting viewpoints. Many researchers proposed, after instructional leadership was deemed the best approach upon its discovery and analysis during the 1970s and '80s, that instructional leadership was insufficient in transforming and motivating staff. Marks and Printy (2003, 372) stated outright that "instructional leadership in practice fell far short of the ideal." Instructional leadership provides a rather limited impact in regard to responding to outside demands of policy, accountability, performativity, and change when used in isolation (Day, Gu, and Sammons 2016, 4). However, it does address the industry context of the educational field. That is why the instructional focus serves as a "how" of educational leadership, and its practices should be viewed and applied in the context of categorization within the transformational framework. The instructional focus is so complex that it is not feasible for one person to handle alone.

The transformational framework combined with an instructional focus is not sufficient, in itself, for creating, implementing, and sustaining the PLC culture. Transformational practices are paramount in establishing a shared leadership environment, although not in themselves sufficient.[88] This insufficiency is largely due to the study of transformational leadership as a model in isolation. However, when viewed with the proper contextual focus (i.e., instructional), it can serve as a sufficient means of establishing the needed foundation for shared leadership.[89] The need for the acquisition of transformational practices with an instructional focus by the qualified central leadership figure provides a logical progression for establishing the intended PLC school culture. The requirement of a shared leadership focus for the creation of the PLC is the logical next step in the progression.

Shared Focus

The shared leadership focus is another "how" used within the transformational framework to create PLCs. Shared leadership is "an overall team environment that consists of three dimensions: shared purpose, social support, and voice" (Carson, Tesluk, and Marrone 2007, 1,218). The pool of research literature on shared leadership uses the terms *shared leadership, collective leadership*, and *distributed leadership* interchangeably. The research on shared leadership's impact in the educational field has yielded contrasting viewpoints. This is largely due to the organizations not adhering to the parameters needed for shared leadership to thrive (Reed and Swaminathan 2016, 4-7).

Organizations attempting to implement shared leadership must ensure, at the least, that principals foster differences and varying opinions, provide clear communication, guarantee that teachers' voices are heard, do not ignore emotions, and clearly define members' roles (Kezar 1998; Beatty 2007; Rice 2006; Hall 2001). The research asserts that leaders must also implement certain norms in regard to group-based teams in order to successfully implement shared leadership (Kocolowski 2010), norms such as "collaborative cultures, the dismantling of teacher isolation, and highly effective teams that focus on learning" (Reed and Swaminathan 2016, 6). Without these parameters and norms, shared leadership can dissolve into groupthink and responsibility dumping, which defeat the intended purposes of the shared focus (Kocolowski 2010, 26).

It has been noted, through examinations of effective implementation of shared leadership, that a qualified central leadership figure is needed to facilitate shared leadership.[90] The behaviors and practices attributed to the effective shared-leadership central figures in educational settings mirror the transformational and instructional behaviors aforementioned. Due to the complexity of implementing the required parameters, which largely focus on the relational aspects of leadership, shared leadership cannot thrive or be sustained without transformational practices, although high-functioning shared leadership requires additional leadership practice focuses.[91] It is unlikely that all of these parameters will be implemented by a leader utilizing the prescribed generic, business-like model of transformational leadership. They would lack the pedagogical, content, or contextual knowledge needed to provide the intellectual stimulation required by the followers in the field of education. While the leader would be able to provide the individual consideration, the lack of intellectual stimulation would prove problematic, as evidenced by the research on transformational leadership practices, which, in the educational environment, tend to yield "small indirect influence on academic or social student outcomes" (Robinson, Lloyd, and Rowe 2008, 639). Additionally, instructional practices, while addressing the intellectual stimulation, lack the individual considerations that tend to inspire and motivate followers.[92] Thus, the instructional leader would lack the converse of the transformational leader. Though the measured impacts are higher for the instructional leader, the limitations for sustaining inspiration and transformation are clear. Thus, the parameters and norms needed for shared leadership require a leader with a mastery of the transformational framework that encompasses instructionally focused practices. The shared construct serves as the foundation for the PLC, and yet, in order to make the transition from shared construct to the PLC culture, additional practices are needed.

Professional Learning Community Focus

The PLC is based on the reciprocal learning and leading of its members; therefore, leadership and responsibilities have to be distributed among staff in order to foster the continuous reciprocating culture. The professional learning community school leader will need the transformational framework along with the previously mentioned practice focuses (instructional and shared) in order to create, implement, and sustain the environment. The PLC expands the shared construct by not only sharing the leadership tasks and roles with a few followers but also supporting "team members who regularly collaborate toward continued improvement in meeting learner needs through a shared curricular-focused vision. Facilitating this effort are (1) supportive leadership and structural conditions; (2) collective challenging, questioning, and reflecting on team-designed lessons; and (3) instructional practices/experiences and team decisions on essential learning outcomes and intervention/enrichment activities based on results of common formative student assessments" (Brown 2016, 8).

The leader will need to utilize the aforementioned skill focuses (i.e., instructional, shared, etc.) to ensure that staff are empowered with the needed pedagogical knowledge and skills, understand and support the shared vision, and believe that the students they are working with can achieve.[93] The specific leadership practices that fortify a PLC environment are balanced between the pedagogical and relational needs of the building stakeholders. The leader must have a clear understanding of the needs of the building stakeholders in order to ensure that the supports and resources provided are directly aligned. The initial end goal of the PLC structure provides stability within the school setting and establishes a positive learning environment that is flexible enough to adjust to future internal and external (when appropriate) pressures.

The identification, analysis, and understanding of skill combinations of the transformational framework with instructional, shared, and PLC focuses can provide the educational leader with the knowledge base needed for the PLC structure. However, the knowledge alone is not enough to create, implement, and sustain the PLC culture.

Enabling the Leader

While it was once believed that great leaders were born with the needed traits and skills to lead and that this pool of natural leaders was limited, our understanding of leadership has since grown. It is now understood, through examples, experience, and research, that leaders can be cultivated. Carraway (1990, 22) surmised the process to be gradual and said that "one can increase their effectiveness in leadership roles through education, training, and development." This simplistic summation, while true, has proven problematic when it comes to the development of educational leaders. The means by which principals have been trained has not led to the type of leadership any industry would pride themselves on. Jacobson et al. (2007, 4) stated that "many [qualified candidates] elect to remain in the classroom where they can retain the security afforded by tenure, a benefit not available to most school administrators." While it is argued that the role changes, responsibilities, and increased accountability have curtailed the interest of qualified principal candidates, even if these persons would step up, their ability to actually lead would still be impaired.

Heystek (2007, 4) said, "This new label denoting a shift to leadership is supposed to be suggestive of a political empowering of principals (Gunter 2004, 21), but in actual practice, they remain bound by the centralized directives through policies, guidelines, accountability measures, and public expectations." The goal of creating PLCs requires not only certain leadership skills but system parameters that currently are not uniformly in place. Clear direction, policy alignment, and proper preparation can improve the development of qualified educational leaders.

One Direction

The suggestion of schools moving in one direction is not in regard to the leader; instead, it refers to the formation of school communities that can outlast the leader.[94] The lack of consensus as to what education should look like further supports the need for the PLC structure as a national minimum standard, since the PLC structure allows for the varied priorities of each school's community. The PLC structure is such that while all schools would foster leading and learning, shared responsibilities, parent engagement, community partnerships, and incorporation of the local community's values and expectations, the uniqueness of each PLC would reflect the variances of the particular communities. Consider the concept of gumbo. While all gumbo requires a broth as the base of the concoction, thus allowing for it to be classified as gumbo, the additional ingredients used reflect the preferences of the palates being served. Thus the chef adds the contents desired by its consumers.

The same is true with the PLC. The basic structure could be the same (broth base), but the content, curriculum, strategy focus, etc., (additional ingredients) would vary based on the needs of the respective school communities (palates). And like the gumbo, the PLC structure allows for experimentation by inclusion of additional ingredients, with the local stakeholders as the judge of its palatability. All the while, every PLC can be evaluated based on the functionality of its structure (i.e., stakeholder satisfaction) as well as its results (i.e., academic performance).

This type of directionizing can set the foundation for educational reform while maintaining the needed local autonomy to ensure that the specific needs of the students can be met. With a specific structural destination in mind, districts can then enhance the enablement of their leaders through policy alignment.

Policy Alignment

What truly perpetuates the enabling of leadership in the school building is the alignment of district policies with the purposes of leadership.[95] Each district will need to examine the intricacies of their policy creation and/or revision if they indeed desire the PLC culture for their district's schools. The creation or reforming of policies that place power in the hands of building leaders can often make the difference in a school's success. Rautiola (2009, 24–25) asserted that "a district's leadership and district organizational conditions are a strong indicator of school leader efficacy. District leaders [need to] primarily create working conditions that are aligned, trusting, share clarity of values, focus on the future, and are conducive to supporting leader efficacy, which impacts teachers' efficacy, leading to student performance." Research has given some fundamental policy changes that can be referred to as "mandatory" for PLC implementation.

Policy change suggestions need to address the new structure of the PLC culture. The push for a professional learning community culture requires changes in principal evaluation policies. Shared structures encourage the sharing of the responsibilities of leadership, but most of the current evaluation policies still hold the principal solely responsible.[96] A means of sharing accountability as well as leadership is needed. As teachers are being called upon to share in the leadership load and responsibilities of the new school structure, policies should not only acknowledge their contribution but also hold them accountable. This type of policy alignment not only empowers teachers but also encourages and enables principals to relinquish impactful responsibilities. As it stands, in many cases, principals are being asked to share leadership, but they are still solely responsible for results. While, theoretically, this shared process is ideal, pragmatically, principals may be reluctant to actually place their careers in the hands of the unaccountable, especially when neither the principal nor the staff has the authority to make major changes.

The need for building autonomy for the principal and subsequently for other building leaders is imperative. The PLC environment focuses on the needs of the immediate school community, thus policies that allow for leader autonomy are needed. Leaders must have the freedom to do what their school community requires.[97] Traditional, top-down decision-making is outdated (Parsons and Beauchamp 2012; Sizemore 1983). Allowing autonomy for buildings to improve does not strip the district of power. To the contrary, a policy change would allow the building to move in the direction it deems best for its population while the district supports it, as needed, and ultimately can intervene if improvements cannot be demonstrated. This would not be an altogether new approach; some districts have already shifted to allowing some decisions to be made at the local building level. The big difference is that autonomy is allowed as part of a process rather than being the process itself. Leaders would not simply be allowed to "run wild." As Sizemore (1983, 22) suggested thirty-five years ago, districts can "provide probation-ary periods for principals and decentralize more authority at the building level for veterans but monitor these principals' performances in elevating achievement." The alignment of district policies with needed building autonomy also requires understanding that change takes time.

Policies should reflect the time it takes to change build-ing culture and improve schools. The processes of culture change, turnaround, and reform require time. Leader hiring and evaluation policies should reflect the acknowledgment of this implementation time. Hiring policies should reflect the identification of candidates with the skills, belief, and knowledge that supports PLC creation, implementation, and sustaining.[98] It is not necessary that the candidates have all the experiences, because leadership is built through said experiences, but a possession of the knowledge should be a minimum requirement when reforming hiring policies. This minimum threshold can decrease the learning curve of the change process.[99]

The evaluation policies should also reflect a focus on the practices that foster PLC environments and account for the necessary, general time frames needed to see results. Additionally, hiring and evaluation policies should reflect the needed time for culture change and improvements. Generally speaking, two to three years and four to five years are needed to turn around elementary and secondary schools, respectively. While some could argue that this type of time frame could put current students at risk, current structures and policies have arguably already done so. Besides, districts would still retain authority to intervene when progress is not demonstrated. Subsequently, districts will need effective means for measuring school progress.

The identification of alternative means of determining school success is needed. Federal and state mandates have constructed achievement measurements largely based on testing or "academic gains." Districts and policymakers need to identify additional and/or alternative means of measuring school success. The antiquated, corporate-like means of using achievement data alone does not properly reflect the multiple impacts of the PLC school culture or the education process itself. The PLC fosters a holistic approach to student growth, and evaluation policies should look to include the ethical, social, and emotional aspects of student growth. Measurement tools for an improved culture, staff impacts, and stakeholder involvement, which individually have been proven to impact student achievement, should be developed through policy reform as well.[100]

Proper Preparation

The last aspect of enabling the building leader is proper preparation. This aspect is listed last, not because of a lack of priority but because it leads into the secondary purpose of this volume: means and tools for leader preparation. Mendez-Morse (1992, 9) explained a perspective on this dilemma by stating, "Unfortunately, accompanying the calls for reform in school systems is an underlying assumption that the leadership needed to execute these changes will somehow emerge." There is a large amount of research and practitioner-based criticism of principal preparation programs.

Whether the programs are university-led or district-led, the overwhelming sentiment is that principals are not ready when they are hired.[101] The expectations are that at least program participants be able to understand and manage the various aspects of the principal's job. School and student data suggest this minimum threshold has yet to be met consistently on a national level. The blame cannot be placed solely on preparatory programs, as the issues of inefficient leader preparation are multifaceted. The lack of clear job expectations, exposure to specific needed skills and practices, and viable tools for practitioners are issues that both preparatory programs and hiring districts share responsibility for.

Clear Expectations

Preparing school leaders, as mentioned previously, requires setting clear expectations.[102] Training principals to "move schools forward," "prepare students for the twenty-first century," or any other ambiguous goal does not provide the clarity needed for adequate principal preparation. With the lack of clarity combined with the ever-changing role of the job, it is no wonder that principals are not prepared for even the minimum job expectations, let alone true leadership. Clear expectation setting should be the role of districts; however, it appears that districts are depending on preparatory programs to have understanding and clarity about what principals should know, and this has not been the case.

The end goal of creating PLC school environments addresses this conundrum. First, it sets a clear direction for where principals should be moving their buildings. In addition, it allows for the infusion, if applicable to the school's environment and vision, of any role change or district expectations. With this type of direction set, preparatory programs could more easily align their programs to meet internal and external expectations associated with educational leadership roles. By setting the establishment of the PLC environment as the national reform norm, preparatory programs could increase the viable applicant pool, as the skills and practices taught would be normalized, allowing for more transient hiring. No longer would principal preparatory programs be so extremely varied in their approaches to preparing principals;

instead, their programs would focus on ensuring that principals are exposed to the skills and practices needed for reaching the goal of establishing PLC schools.

Exposure to Needed Skills/Practices

Preparation of the school leader is dependent on the leader's knowledge and understanding of the skills and practices needed to meet the expectations of the district for which they work. With a new, universal, and clarified expectation that principals understand how to go about creating, implementing, and sustaining professional learning community school environments, the functioning of non-district Principal Preparation Programs (PPP) could be sustained. As noted previously, this knowledge is based on the concept that the educational leader must possess a basic foundation of leadership skills that can be applied to various situations. Transformational practices, namely, the Five Leadership Practices identified by Kouzes and Posner, would provide the leader with a leadership practice framework that would encompass the needed subsequent focuses and foster the creation of professional learning communities.[103] This framework provides the simplest means of integrating supporting focuses, as will be described later. However, it is clear that transformational practices alone would not be enough to generate sustained academic achievement, let alone create, implement, and sustain PLCs.

An instructional practice focus can yield a 4 percent higher achievement rate than can transformational practices alone.[104] Instructionally focused leadership practices, categorized within the transformational framework, would provide the industry-specific focus needed by the principal. A leader solely focused on instructional leadership may have an unbalanced leadership approach, but with the leader's understanding of how such practices fall within the transformational framework, they are more equipped to maintain balanced leadership than if they were to view the knowledge of instructional practices in isolation. With all the pressures placed on educational leaders, transforming a school and maintaining a balance of leadership could be problematic for any one individual. Implementing the shared leadership focused practices provides workload relief and is a catalyst for cultivating a professional learning community.

Distributed leadership practices, when implemented properly, can have an even greater impact on achievement than any one leadership style (Robinson, Lloyd, and Rowe 2008, 24). However, in order for distributed leadership to work, certain norms and expectations must be set. Transformational practices with an instructional focus would well equip the newly trained educational leader to properly implement and maintain a distributed leadership style in their building, all with the expectation of creating, implementing, and sustaining a PLC.

The professional-learning-community-focused practices entail the leader establishing, modeling, and promoting certain parameters and norms that foster "creating and sharing knowledge" (Fullan 2002, 4). The PLC practices "transform the teaching force, [. . .] reduce teacher workload, foster increased teacher ownership, and create the capacity to manage change in a sustainable way" and can only be sustained with the pre-establishment of the transformational framework that encompasses the instructional and shared practices (Fullan 2002, 2). This is the culminating practice focus that sets the school leadership in position to "adapt [their] style to the unique characteristics and demands of the [school] community" (Niece 1993, 4). With all of the practice focuses aforementioned, the importance of balancing practice implementation is key.

Balance of Practices

In addition to the knowledge of the needed skills, the importance of maintaining a balance of practices must be stressed. Maintaining a balance of the overarching, transformational framework practice areas is important for sustaining effective leadership and the PLC. The focus areas (vision, modeling, enabling, etc.) are the suggested foundation of the transformational framework, and thus, an imbalance of the practices can result in the instability of the organization. Proper balance between the relational and task-oriented practices must be maintained. As seen in figure 1, the imbalance of any one of the five focus areas can have detrimental impacts on the other four (Guilford 2017, 83).

Figure 1: Impact of Imbalance of Leadership Practices Matrix

	Inspire Shared Vision	Model the Way	Challenge the Process	Enable Others to Act	Encourage the Heart
w/o Inspiring Shared Vision	N/A	Behaviors modeled are not aligned to any unifying purpose.	Challenges are not aligned to any unifying purpose.	Enabling becomes random and ambiguous because actions are not aligned to any unifying purpose.	Motivation focuses on random tasks and lacks an end point because they are not aligned to any unifying purpose.
w/o Modeling the Way	Leadership becomes authoritarian as the efforts toward the vision are only performed by followers, and undermines the vision because leader appears unwilling or unable to perform desired behaviors.	N/A	Challenging is not viewed as an acceptable practice, as the leader does not demonstrate the attribute.	Follower perceptions of the leader can be construed as "talk, but cannot walk," and leadership becomes authoritarian as the efforts toward the vision are only performed by followers.	Unsustainable since the leader is unwilling to demonstrate commitment to the vision through modeling desired behaviors.

w/o Challenging the Process	Devalues the vision, since the leader is unwilling to "do whatever it takes."	Without modeling how to challenge the status quo, effectively, followers may become hesitant to try new things as the leader has not affirmed the behaviors.	N/A	The leader is perceived as not willing to clear the path for followers to achieve the vision.	Unsustainable due to the nature of change, and eventually, the followers could view the encouragement as a farce since the followers are being asked to take risks the leader is unwilling to take themselves.
w/o Enabling Others to Act	The attainment of the vision becomes impeded, if not impossible, without providing means for followers to act.	Modeling can transform into micromanagement if followers are not free to apply the modeled behaviors (i.e., instructional practices, strategies, etc.)	The risk of challenging the status quo can become obsolete since the followers are not able to act on the vision.	N/A	The encouragement can be viewed as futile since followers are being encouraged to act but do not have the means or ability.
w/o Encouraging the Heart	The vision can become burdensome and followers could lose ownership of their participation in reaching it.	The tone of non-encouragement can be set, since all important behaviors are modeled by the leader.	The risks of the challenge can be increased greatly, since the followers can become discontented, overburdened, and frustrated by the lack of encouragement.	Enablement without acknowledgment or recognition can lead to discontent and frustration due to the lack of encouragement, thus making the progress of the enablement unsustainable.	N/A

The research on instructional leaders highlights the imbalance of the sole use of instructional practices, which limit instructional leadership's relational and motivational impact and sustainability. The critical need for balance in leadership practice implementation has spurred the rallying cry for "integrated" models by some researchers.[105] The call for an integrated model acknowledges the limitations of instructional practices in isolation when it comes to sustained school improvement and turnaround. The instructional practices lend themselves to three, sometimes four, of the Five Leadership Practices areas, thus limiting the impacts of the relational elements of leadership. Even with this type of skill knowledge, it is imperative that potential education leaders be provided with the means of skill implementation.

Tools for Implementation

With so much research knowledge about practices and their effectiveness, preparatory programs will need to provide tangible means for participants to categorize, experiment with, and evaluate new practices.

Categorization Tool

The five practices of exemplary leaders by Kouzes and Posner is the recommended transformational framework in which instructional, shared, and PLC practices can be categorized (Quin et al. 2015, 1). The transformational framework serves as the "what" leaders are doing; they are transforming their building into professional learning communities. Instructionally focused practices can be categorized under one of the Five Leadership Practices (transformational framework). Instructional practices serve as the "how" leaders will transform the educational setting, which in turn can facilitate shared leadership implementation. Shared leadership is an additional "how" educational leaders can transform. The shared leadership components and parameters can be categorized under one of the Five Leadership Practices as well. Additionally, the practices that specifically foster the PLC culture can be categorized under one of the Five Leadership Practices. Figure 2 is an example of the type of categorization tool leaders could utilize. Once the program participants have the tools needed to organize the various leadership practices they are exposed to, they will need the knowledge and tools to experiment with implementation.

Figure 2: Example Instructional, Shared and PLC Practices Categorization Matrix

5 Leadership Practices (Transformational Leadership)	Inspire a Shared Vision	Model the Way	Challenge the Process	Enable Others to Act	Encourage the Heart
Instructional Focus Practices	Setting school academic goals Setting standards for achievement/ setting tone for learning climate	Monitoring achievement levels/ evaluating programs		Protecting instructional time and programs Hiring, supervising, evaluating teachers Maximizing effects of instructional organization	
Shared Focus Key Components, Indicators & Education Findings	Shared Purpose Partnership Equity Information about the company and its strategy is shared Involve the team in decision-making	Accountability The work team resolves differences to reach agreement Encourage multiple opinions Clear communication	Decentralized interaction among personnel Teamwork is promoted with team itself Extent of sharing is justified in practice No underestimation of the complexity of shared leadership	Voice Internal team environment and external coaching Joint completion of tasks Mutual skill development Ownership Work is distributed properly to take advantage of members' unique skills The team works together to identify opportunities to improve productivity and efficiency Team leaders should ensure they delegate enough autonomy and responsibility to all members in their team Encourage the team to self-manage its performance to the extent possible Understand individual roles Collegial climate	Social Support Emotional support Embrace principles of fostering differences Emotions cannot be ignored

Professional Learning Community Traits	Learning environment is community centered Look to staff's expertise Regularly collaborate toward continued improvement in meeting learner needs through a shared curricular-focused vision	Recognize the individual needs and desires of their staff Respect staff's expertise Supportive leadership Instructional practices/experiences and team decisions on essential learning outcomes based on the results of common formative student assessments Creating and sharing knowledge	Collective challenging, questioning, and reflecting on team-designed lessons Divert school energy and resources to support the school vision	Recognize the individual needs and desires of their staff Rely on staff to be strong team players Supportive structural conditions Intervention/enrichment activities based on the results of common formative student assessments Peer learning	Staff know that they are a vital part of the whole academic process Building and sustaining positive professional relationships

Enabling Experimentation

This research is not championing any particular leadership model. More so, as suggested by past research, a focus on specific practices that lead to the PLC environment is the purpose. Leadership practices, no matter the type, have been shown to be interpreted in varied manners by followers.[106]

These follower interpretations have been impacted by the leader's age, gender, years of experience, ethnicity, etc. For this reason, and because of the contextual nature of school building composition, no specific set of practices will work for all principals.[107] The Five Leadership Practices provide the universal "what" for all principals. However, the "how'" of instructional, shared, and PLC practices will need to be specific to each school's context. Preparatory programs will need to provide participants with the skills and tools that guide them through the identification and experimentation of selected practices which they choose to implement.[108] This experimentation process should consider factors such as student population, staff composition, grade level, socioeconomic status, etc.

The tools would, after proper practice categorization, allow the leader to pull from their "playbook" the practices most likely to meet their specific leadership task focus (i.e., vision, modeling, enabling, etc.). The preparation of the leader for experimentation with research/evidence-based practices serves a dual purpose: (1) it allows the leader to identify specifically what works in their building for future duplication, and (2) the experimentation serves as a model for the teachers.[109] It should be noted that these principals would be experimenting with proven practices that align with their school's vision and needs. It is not random guessing but rather calculated investigation. The preparation of the leader would be incomplete if they were not also shown how to evaluate the implementation of said practices.

Enable Practice Evaluation

The evaluation of implemented leadership practices by the leader is important. The leader needs to be able to self-monitor the impacts of various practices in order to solidify their "toolbox" of practices for sustained success. The leader's immediate goal is the creation, implementation, and sustaining of the PLC, which, as described earlier, requires the use of practices from varied leadership focus areas. Without immediate and localized knowledge of the practices' impacts, the leader cannot, with any fidelity, determine the practices that are beneficial to their specific building context. Also, this evaluative process provides clarity for the leader about practices that potentially can be used by other leaders in the building and/or future principals, which helps with the leader succession drop-off that occurs in many schools. The last benefit of leader self-evaluation is the modeling of leading and learning for the building followers. The leader, who is championing staff's incorporation of new instructional approaches, would be the leading model of inquiry. In regard to the means of evaluating individual leadership practices implemented, further research and action are needed.

While many leadership practice measurement tools do exist (PIMRS, LPI, etc.), one designed to capture data for varied leadership practices in varied contexts has yet to be discovered by the author. Since the ability to self-evaluate is a skill needed by the leader, the preparatory programs can utilize course development to assist the leader with fine-tuning this skill. Essentially, the preparatory program should focus on exposing the leader to various leadership practice evaluation tools, discussing the needed data points particular leadership practices would require, and practicing the development of multiple tools. This by no means ensures that the tools are scientifically sound; however, the leader would have a better understanding of the skill and could further hone the skill with experience.[110] The initial use (to prevent implementation hesitancy) of some combination of basic Likert Scale questionnaires, follower interviews, school collection means and an evaluative tool is suggested.

The preparation of the leader is not a foolproof process. Even the best preparatory program will have participants that will exit without a full understanding of the process. However, it is believed that by providing clear expectations, exposure to needed skills/practices, and tools for implementation, preparatory programs can make tremendous impacts in the preparation of school leaders.

Tools for Enabling Process

The educational leader will need tangible means to learn the tenets of the Five Leadership Practices and categorize, experiment with, and evaluate researched practices implemented in their building. This preparation is not random or stagnant. Instead, the preparation consists of a logical and mutable process. The preparation process allows the leader to be an active participant in the acquisition and implementation of leadership skills needed to create, implement, and sustain the PLC culture.

The process

The process would consist of intense acquisition of the transformational practices, identification and categorization of research/evidence-based practices that foster the PLC culture, the selection of practices to include in the yearly implementation "snapshot," the setup of implementation and evaluation plans, and the completion of implementation reflections. The purpose of leadership is to lead. Where are the practices leading followers? To create a successful school? What does that look like? For County A, the answer is test scores and attendance. District B wants improved graduation rates and parent involvement. School C wants better essay writing, improved math skills, and STEM focus. So how does preparing leaders with the Five Leadership Practices accomplish this? It doesn't. The practices are too generic, in isolation, to be effective. However, once a clear end goal is set (the creation of the PLC) the practices can be presented as the first step in a process that moves the leader, and subsequently the followers, toward their destination.

Figure 3: Leadership Enabling Process

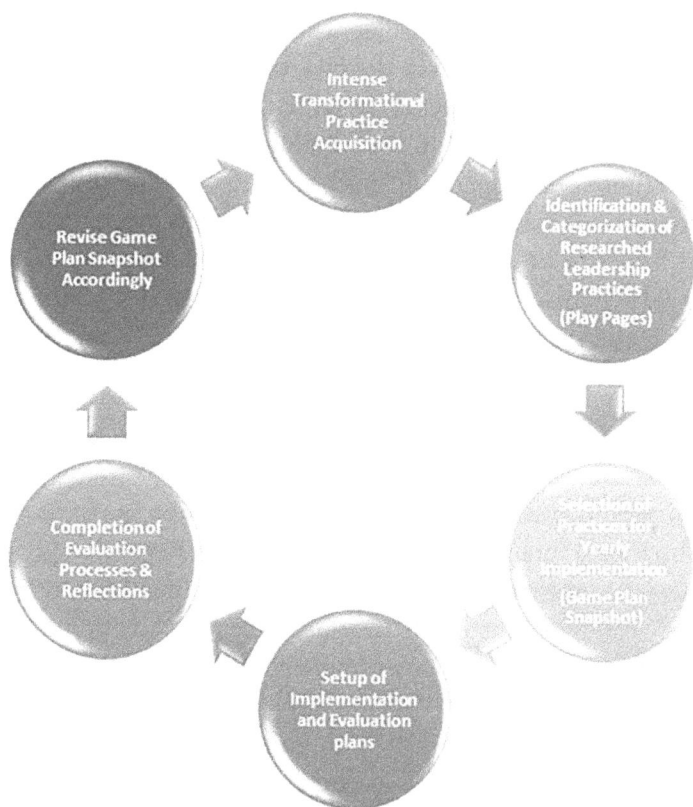

Transformational Practices Acquisition

The acquisition of the transformational leadership practices that will serve as the framework for enabling educational leaders is vital. The use of the Five Leadership Practices by Kouzes and Posner is the most conducive model to utilize. The study of leadership practices by Quin et al. (2015, 1) determined that transformational leadership practices had greater impacts in school settings and even suggested that principal preparation programs utilize Kouzes and Posner's Five Leadership Practices, but the document omitted the means by which to accomplish such a task. This research, while informative and enlightening, still presented the concept of leadership as its own end. The recommended use of the Five Leadership Practices becomes more impactful when viewed as a flexible framework upon which to build. Using the Five Leadership Practices as categories for "what" leaders are doing allows for a simplified contextual adaptation for determining "how" to do it. The preparation of the leader would begin with an intense acquisition of the definitions and purposes of the categories of the transformational framework. This preparation would give leaders a clear understanding of the rationales of each category and their general transformative functioning. Also, leaders would learn how the framework's usage would ultimately lead to the creation and sustaining of professional learning communities. Once this foundational learning had taken place, the leaders would then begin to utilize the framework to identify and categorize potential leadership practices.

Identification and Categorization

The identification of practices can occur through coursework, reading, professional development, seminars, or the like. However, during their initial introduction to the process, leaders would use research materials only under the guidance of their preparation leader. This parameter is similar to the classroom practice of teaching students how to identify reliable as opposed to unreliable sources.[111] Leaders would utilize research journals' articles/documents to first focus on instructional practices. The leader would seek out instructional practices and record the source, practice, grade level studied, and school setting. After identifying feasible instructional practices, the leader participant would then determine which of the five transformational framework areas the practice aligned with. The feasibility and categorization, initially, could be done independently or in the whole group or small groups. This would be determined by the preparation program itself. Next, a Practice Play page for each of the five transformational categories would be created, into which the identified and categorized practices would be entered, as seen in figure 4. The leader would then complete the same process for the shared leadership and professional learning community focuses. The availability of leadership practices for the various transformational framework focus areas is infinite. It should be noted, however, that some practices might be redundant in nature and require the optional further step of consolidation.

Figure 4: Sample Enable Practices Play page

Focus Type	Source	Practice	Study Grade Level	School Setting Studied
Instructional	Aitken (2009, 1)	Create the processes and structures that enable the participants to focus on teaching and learning.	High School	Varied
PLC	Aitken (2009, 3)	Set up circumstances where teachers can experience important results.	High School	Varied
PLC	Aitken (2009, 6)	Support and develop teachers.	High School	Varied
PLC	Aitken (2009, 6)	Create and implement structures or organizational processes that directly align to the school's vision.	High School	Varied
Shared	Allen, Grigsby, and Peters (2015, 4)	Exhibit collaborative decision-making.	Elementary	Small, suburban, southeast, Texas schools
Instructional	Allen, Grigsby, and Peters (2015, 4)	Remove obstacles that prohibit teachers from focusing on instruction.	Elementary	Small, suburban, southeast, Texas schools

Game Plan Snapshot

The next step is for the leader to select two to three practices per framework area (i.e., vision, model, etc.) that are conducive to and aligned with the school's vision for implementation. The specific building context comes into play at this point. The practices selected should be based on the leader's understanding of the needs of the building. To determine such, the leader may use surveys, interviews, or other evaluation means for obtaining the current state of their building. A process similar to that illustrated in figure 5 may be apt for diagnosing and determining needed practices. These reflections would guide the leader in their selection of the practices for their Game Plan Snapshot that are specific to the contextual needs of their school. The selected practices (keeping in mind the need for balance) can then be placed into the yearly Game Plan Snapshot for easy reference and focus, as seen in figure 6. With the Game Plan Snapshot in place, the leader would be ready to begin setting up practice implementation and evaluation, which is Step Four of the Leadership Enabling Process.

Figure 5: Example School Climate/ Context Reflections

Step 1	Step 2	Step 3
Ask: Is there a school vision?	Ask: Has modeling been established in the school's culture?	Ask: Is there evidence of the school (curriculum, programs, etc.) challenging the status quo?

If "yes"—
• Does the vision reflect belief in all students' achievement?
• Does the vision have support from all stakeholders?
  o If not, why not?
• Does the vision reflect leader's beliefs?
  o If not, why not?
	If "yes"—
	• Staff should be able to explain areas in which modeling is present.
	• Determine whether current modeling practices are aligned with vision.
	  o If "yes"—
	    ▪ Continue current modeling, and add to modeled practices.
		If "yes"—
		• Identify where "challenging" exists,
		  o continue fostering, look for innovative practices of building upon them, and
		  o identify new areas to challenge that alignment with vision.

If "yes" Options— • Alter vision to adhere to all requirements. • Create new vision (potentially set back established progress). • Adhere to current vision, with plans for future revisions.	If "no"— • Model program offerings' alignment to vision. • Model curriculum alignment to program offerings and vision. • Model instructional practices to curriculum, program offerings, and vision. • Establish and model rules and procedures that align to vision.	If "no"— • Identify practices of challenging the status quo that are aligned with the vision. • Foster them and look for innovative practices of building upon them.

If "no"— • Gain building feed-back for vision. • Create vision that reflects belief in all students' achievement. • Communicate vision. • Foster staff commit-ment to shared vision.		
Step 4	**Step 5**	
Ask: Are all stakeholders enabled to perform their respective tasks in regard to the school's vision?	Ask: Are all stakeholders being encouraged and inspired to perform their respective tasks that foster the school's vision?	
If "yes"— • Identify the practices of enabling enabled stakeholders and practices of fostering future enablement.	If "yes"— • Identify current/past prac-tices of encouragement. • Determine effectiveness of current/past practices of encouragement. • Continue and/or improve on current/past practices of encouragement. • Look for new practices of building on current effective encouragement.	
If "no"— • Identify stake-holders and their respective tasks. • Identify practices of enabling (needs) stakeholders to complete their tasks. • Plan for enablement. • Enable. • Identify (even antic-ipate) future needs (based on vision needs) and prac-tices of enabling.	If "no"— • Identify stakeholders and their respective tasks. • Identify practices of encouragement. • Implement encour-agement practices. • Determine effectiveness of encouragement practices. • Look for new practices of building on current effective encouragement.	

Figure 6: Sample Game Plan Snapshot

5 Leadership Practices (Transformational Framework)	Inspire a Shared Vision	Model the Way	Challenge the Process	Enable Others to Act	Encourage the Heart
Instructional Focus Practices	Set school academic goals	Monitor achievement levels/evaluate programs		Protect instructional time and programs	
Shared Focus **Key components, indicators & education findings**	Shared Purpose Partnership	Encourage multiple opinions Clear communication	Decentralize personnel	Joint completion of tasks Mutual skill development Understand individual roles	Emotional support Embrace principles of fostering differences

71

Implementation and Evaluation Plan Setup

As mentioned, the leader will need a means of documenting the implementation and evaluation of selected practices in order to gauge effectiveness within their school building. After selecting the specific practices they intend to implement in the school, the leader would prepare an implementation and evaluation document similar to figure 7. The document requires the leader to record pertinent information prior to implementation.

The initial seven sections of the tool describe the practice in detail and culminate with a rationale for implementation. After describing the practice and the reason for its use, the leader then provides a breakdown of the steps they will take to implement the practice. This section requires the leader to demonstrate an understanding of the practice and context in which leaders operate. In addition to fostering intentional and logical implementation of practices, the implementation details allow the leader to effectively reflect upon the completion of the process.

After determining means of implementation, the leader is required to identify a means of assessing the practice implementation. This does not have to be a complex process. The use of both quantitative and qualitative data is suggested, as the combination tends to provide a more holistic view. The use of simple Likert Scale questionnaires, short-response question sets, student data, staff data, interviews, or a combination of means can all provide valuable feedback for the leader.

Once the evaluation means is determined and created, the leader would then fully implement the practice. The length of the implementation is at the discretion of the leader, or the collective leadership group responsible for leadership practice monitoring in the PLC. Following the implementation period, the leader would analyze their data to determine the effectiveness of the practice. Subsequently, recommendations for future practice use would be recorded, and finally, the leader would attach all documents used during the Implementation and Evaluation Plan (i.e., original practice source document, evaluation tools, data sources, etc.). The Implementation and Evaluation Plans can be reused in the future, and the abundance of details can only serve to improve future implementation attempts. Lastly, the plan can be shared with other building leaders or colleagues to add to the playbook.

Figure 7: Sample Leadership Practice Implementation and Evaluation Tool

Leadership Role:	Leadership Practice Focus:
Practice Source:	Practice:
Implementation Dates:	Intended Impacted Population:
Practice Implementation Rationale (the need and reasoning for practice choice):	
Implementation Steps Performed	

1.	Date Performed:
2.	Date Performed:

Data Sources Used for Evaluation (Likert Scale questionnaires, follower interviews, school data, etc.):
Implementation Conclusions (include written and numeric results):
Recommendations for Future Use of Practice:
List and Attachments of All Supporting Documents:

Discussion and Conclusion

Discussion

Clearly, a lot of work needs to be done to improve our public education system. Research experts, consultants, and other outsiders have proposed various means of fixing our schools, but few of these approaches have sustained success, largely due to a lack of adherence to the specific school building contexts. Instead of these programs adjusting to the building contexts, many force the building context to conform to its framework. While there are many models and programs that foster a shared leadership environment, the author has yet to see a comprehensive approach that addresses not only the building culture but also the practices the building leader would need, the tools that would enable the leader, and the responsibilities of the district to foster the changes.

By no means is the information presented new. On the contrary, the information dates back decades. However, the perspective through which it is viewed and presented is different. Rather than seeking a specific model concept, the analysis of past leadership research suggested a different approach. The search for major themes of past and present research led to the recognition of the benefits of professional learning communities as the most effective means of sustainable school improvement. The random analysis of the best leadership practices is obsolete without goal clarification.

Turning schools around and improving academic achievement are reflective of a limited vision for the purposes of schooling. These limited viewpoints and expectations are not shared by school staff, because teachers believe their students are more than grades and scores, and they desire the type of vision and leadership that support these beliefs. The PLC culture is not intended only for struggling schools. The PLC structure fosters higher expectations than even those of schools that have garnered the status of "successful schools" under the current data-driven evaluation processes. The culture change would raise the bar of expectation for all schools, both struggling and successful.

There is no argument that the improvement of public schools is a complex task. However, by implementing a normative culture that is flexible and adaptable to change, we can simplify the process and focus on the task that really makes a difference: meeting our students' needs.

Conclusion

Public school reform has been an ongoing process in the United States for at least the past four decades. The focus of reform has largely revolved around curriculum content, accountability, and measurements. These efforts, while commendable, have resulted in the mediocre, at best, current state of US public school performance. No matter what improvements are suggested by experts and policymakers, the fact remains that no sweeping changes will occur without proper school structuring and subsequent leadership development. Effective school building leadership is critical in sustaining any reform efforts, and the research has been championing this perspective for decades. However, as noted, the training of educational leaders to lead followers toward abstract and ambiguous goals has not worked. The establishment of clear and concise goals is imperative to the development and effectiveness of educational leaders. The creation, implementation, and sustaining of professional learning community environments as the immediate goal for educational leaders provides such clarity. In addition, by focusing principal preparatory programs on teaching the specific skills needed to implement the PLC culture, providing the tools for implementation and evaluation, and altering policy to support the culture change, we can increase the viable pool of leaders willing to take on the task.

The reform we seek will not occur by adding new parts to a faulty structure. The establishment of a new structure is required. The addition of the latest "cookbook" or "rapid turnaround" processes is the equivalent of adding a new level or addition on a home structure that should have been condemned and demolished years before. To further the analogy, this is in no means a criticism of the construction workers (teachers), as they are under the strict direction of the engineers (policymakers) and general contractors (district). The workers may voice their concerns, but the remodeling proceeds. Initially, from the outside, it appears beautiful and safe, but all involved know the faulty foundation on which the renovations were built. The time has come for a stoppage of such dangerous, wasteful, and unsustainable approaches. A clearing of the old structure and an establishment of a new building is needed—one that can sustain the now and the future. The process is not simple, but the choice to begin *is*. If education is based on the use of research/evidence-based practices and data, then maybe it is time to stop and listen to what the research has been saying for the past fifty years. We can do it, All Together Now.

Endnotes

[1] A national average of 75 percent of twelfth grade students performed below proficiency in math, and 63 percent performed below proficiency in English in 2015 (US Department of Education, Institute of Education Sciences, National Center for Education Statistics, National Assessment of Educational Progress (NAEP) n.d.). From 1992 to 2015 the national average twelfth grade reading assessment scores remained below proficient, while the same demographic's math scores remained well below proficiency between 2005 and 2015 (US Department of Education, Institute of Education Sciences, National Center for Education Statistics, National Assessment of Educational Progress (NAEP) n.d.). As of 2017, 60 percent of fourth graders, 66 percent of eighth graders, and 75 percent of twelfth graders performed below proficiency on the math NEAP assessment (National Center for Education Statistics (NCES) n.d.). NEAP reading assessment proficiencies were not much better, with 63 percent, 64 percent, and 63 percent of students less than proficient, respectively (National Center for Education Statistics (NCES) n.d.).

[2] Green (2010, 63), in reference to the No Child Left Behind Act, refuted the sole use of standardized test scores as a means of gauging school efficiency. Lock and Lummis (2014) cited Wise (1978) who stated "Hyper–Rationalisation and, in doing so, refuted the worth of minimum competency testing and the narrowing of educational goals."

[3] The problem with this dependency is the misinterpretation of research, ambiguous findings, and "weak research designs" (Hallinger, Bickman, and Davis 1996).

[4] Leech and Fulton (2008, 2, 5) state, "Supporters of reform movements have proposed that public schools' structures and processes be changed." The same text also suggests that "to create lasting change, there must be a change in governance through a redistribution of power and control." Shifts of power are met with strong resistance and allow for continued debate.

[5] The development and maintenance of "decentralization policies" is the opposite of what happens in the current public school system (Fullan 2002). This is true even with some systems dictating the use of pseudo-shared leadership, as these directives are top-down, which "contrasts sharply with the certainty of agencies that sanction, regulate, and administer educational leadership" (Parsons & Beauchamp 2012, 4).

[6] Balyer (2012) stated that the educational leader had to be adaptable to an ever-changing society and equipped with the skills to address all the aspects of the school building.

[7] "Cookbook approaches to training packages that limit opportunities for principals to adapt research findings to their settings are, therefore, likely to be counterproductive (Barth 1990; Hallinger 1992; Marsh 1992)" (Hallinger, Bickman, and Davis 1996, 18).

[8] External pressures; need for executing managerial, instructional and relational tasks; and high demands for effectiveness in a complex position have led to the push for shared/collaborative approaches to leadership (Gautam, Alford, and Khanal 2015; Halverson, Kelley, and Shaw 2014; Lambert 2002; Tatlah et al. 2014).

[9] The leader as a facilitator of learning and collaboration for the building and staff has been demonstrated as the most effective means for sustained improvement (Aitken 2009; Crow 2007; Leithwood and Sun 2012).

[10] "The research also indicates that a district's leadership and district organizational conditions are a strong indicator of school leader efficacy. District leaders [need to] primarily create working conditions that are aligned, trusting, share clarity of values, focus on the future and are conducive to supporting leader efficacy, which impacts teachers' efficacy, leading to student performance" (Rautiola 2009, 24–25).

[11] Mendez-Morse (1992, 23), while examining leadership traits that lead to school change, noted the "effective schools movement" that focused on low-income, high-minority schools that had abnormal success.

[12] For more takeaways from the studies conducted on the effective urban schools review, see Edmonds (1979), Sizemore (1983), and Weber (1987).

[13] Notably, Edmonds (1979) and Niece (1993) identified the omission of key relational traits by the principals and school characteristics of the urban schools being examined. When these omissions are combined with the commonly noted leader traits and culture characteristics, the presence of professional learning communities becomes evident.

[14] Edmonds (1979), Krug (1990), Mendez-Morse (1992), and Sizemore (1983) provide a combined listing of all of the omitted and reported principal traits and building culture characteristics.

[15] Historical contexts for post-desegregation urban school environments was examined using data/information from Baker, Myers, and Vasquez (2014) and Thompson (2017). The connections to PLCs and leadership refer back to the previously mentioned Mendez-Morse (1992).

[16] For more about elements, structures, and needed parameters of professional learning communities, examine Gautam, Alford, and Khanal (2015), Jacobson et al. (2007), and Lambert (2007).

[17] Explanations for the importance of localization, stakeholders, and community beliefs incorporation were extracted from Gantner, Newsom, and Dunlap (2000), Koonce and Hanes (2012), and Mendez-Morse (1992).

[18] Brown (2016), Gautam, Alford, and Khanal (2015), and Liu (2013) each note the need for the distinction between PLCs and shared leadership. The distinction is even more pertinent now with the implementation of pseudo-shared leadership, where the needed cultural parameters are not fostered, and thus the results are not sustainable.

[19] A general understanding of the shared leadership model can be gleaned from Halverson, Kelley, and Shaw (2014), Frey and Fisher (2013), and Harnack and Seebaum (2016).

[20] The "barriers" of socioeconomic status, minority status, lack of belief in students, and all others are negated by the localized efforts fostered

by the PLC culture (Edmonds 1979; Sizemore 1983; Jacobson et al. 2007).

[21] "Effective principals know they cannot go it alone. [. . .] Instead, they make good use of all the skills and knowledge on the faculty and among others, encouraging the many capable adults who make up a school community to step into leadership roles and responsibilities" (Mendels 2012, 3).

[22] Citing Aieta, Barth, and O'Brien (1988, 19): "Effective principals in the year 2000 will have to be the kinds of people who can recognize and utilize alternative leadership hierarchies, rather than try to be all things to all people. [. . .] The principal must be the builder of a community of leaders within the school" (Portin, 5).

[23] For more on the cited benefits of the PLC structure, see Aitken (2009), Allen, Grigsby, and Peters (2015), Crow (2007), Korkmaz (2006), Lambert (2002), Louis (2015), and Masumoto and Brown-Welty (2009).

[24] "Leadership focused on the development of teachers' knowledge and skills, professional community and school climate could lead to improved student academic performance" (Shouppe and Pate, 8).

[25] Multiple research has asserted the importance of these factors, including Edmonds (1979), Day, Gu, and Sammons (2016), Hallinger, Bickman, and Davis (1996), Kantrowitz, Mathews, and Bondy (2007), and Leithwood, Patten, and Jantzi (2010).

[26] Leaders should "[b]uild structures to enable collaboration. Leaders ensure that staff participate in decisions about programs and instruction, establish working conditions that facilitate staff collaboration for planning and professional growth, and distribute leadership broadly among staff" (Leithwood and Sun 2012, 15). Also, "when leadership was shared between teachers and principals, teachers' working relationships were stronger and student achievement was higher" (Leithwood and Sun 2012, 24).

[27] Allen, Grigsby, and Peters (2015, 16, 18) addressed this aspect specifically by stating, "Teachers felt more positive about their school environment when their principal values them as a partner in the school program, and not just as a staff member" and "In addition, administrators can impact school climate when they choose to build trusting,

cooperative relationships with teachers, particularly when they recognize the individual needs and desires of their staff."

[28] Without the needed parameter of open interaction between administration and stakeholders, shared leadership becomes a dumping of responsibilities and tasks, thus creating toxic school cultures (Brown 2016; Fullan 2002; Masumoto and Brown-Welty 2009).

[29] These schools typically have limited resources and poor cultures and are often the starting point for novice teachers, since veterans usually work to avoid such placements (Snipes, Williams, and Petteruti 2006).

[30] True sharing (including the establishment of the needed culture and environment) will lighten this workload since the "notion of efficient leadership has shifted from delegation and direction to collaboration and shared responsibilities (Crowther and Olsen 1997)" (Tatlah et al. 2014, 3).

[31] "Because of strong instructional leadership with a focus on standards and high expectations, leaders and teachers in all three high schools described the departure of some former teachers as 'a good thing' and felt that teacher turnover was not necessarily negative as frequently implied by researchers" (Masumoto and Brown-Welty 2009, 11).

[32] "Effective principals know they cannot go it alone. [. . .] Instead, they make good use of all the skills and knowledge on the faculty and among others, encouraging the many capable adults who make up a school community to step into leadership roles and responsibilities [. . .] researchers found, noting that the school leaders they observed 'consistently expressed' the desire to see teachers working, teaching, and helping one another" (Mendels 2012, 3). "Teachers who are more committed to the values of an organization and to its members are more likely to adopt instructional practices recommended by the organization, assist colleagues, and work harder to achieve organizational goals" (Ross and Gray 2006, 5).

[33] Kocolowski, M. (2010). *Shared leadership: Is it time for a change? Emerging Leadership Journeys*, 3(1), 22–32.

[34] Teacher rationales were extracted from Sutcher, L., Darling-Hammond, L., and Carver-Thomas, D. (2016). *A coming crisis in teaching? Teacher supply, demand, and shortages in the US*. Palo Alto, CA: Learning Policy Institute.

[35] "When teachers believe their principal exhibit a high level of idealized attributes, they identify better with their leader and thus leads them to feel more positive about the overall climate of the campus" (Allen, Grigsby, and Peters 2015, 15). In their study findings, Leech and Fulton (2008) cited that Smylie (1992) "found teachers appeared to be more involved in school decision-making if their relationship with the school principal was perceived to be 'open, collaborative, facilitative, and supportive' (p. 63)" (339).

[36] See the full paper for more details: Hoy, A. W. (2000). Changes in teacher efficacy. Paper presented at Annual Meeting of the American Educational Research Association, New Orleans, LA.

[37] "Principals who encourage the development of teacher strengths can motivate teachers to try new instructional strategies" (Allen, Grigsby, and Peters 2015, 17).

[38] Mendels (2012, 56) cited Stanford University education policy analyst Linda Darling-Hammond, "'The number one reason for teachers' decisions about whether to stay in a school is the quality of administrative support—and it is the leader who must develop this organization' (Darling-Hammond 2007, 17)."

[39] For detailed analyses of teacher concerns and reported needs, see Snipes, Williams, and Petteruti (2006). *Critical trends in urban education: Sixth survey of America's great city schools.* Northwest, DC: Council of the Great City Schools, *and* Sutcher, L., Darling-Hammond, L., and Carver-Thomas, D. (2016). *A coming crisis in teaching? Teacher supply, demand, and shortages in the US.* Palo Alto, CA: Learning Policy Institute.

[40] The constant role changes for principals, combined with the multifaceted responsibilities, leads to this sporadic implementation (Gantner, Newsom, and Dunlap 2000; Harnack and Seebaum 2016; Lashway 2003).

[41] The culture shift and subsequent responsibility-sharing affords administration more time for staff development, and thus increases the ability of staff to take on even more leadership (Brown 2016; Gautam, Alford, and Khanal 2015; Lambert 2002).

[42] "A professional learning community is made up of team members who regularly collaborate toward continued improvement in meeting learner needs through a shared curricular-focused vision. Facilitating

this effort are (1) supportive leadership and structural conditions; (2) collective challenging, questioning, and reflecting on team-designed lessons; and (3) instructional practices/experiences and team decisions on essential learning outcomes and intervention/enrichment activities based on results of common formative student assessments" (Brown 2016, 8).

43 "Some authors have suggested that professional communities are most likely to develop when teachers interact seriously with new information obtained through professional development, reading groups or action research (Louis and Leithwood 1998; Schon 1987; Scribner et al. 1999; Scribner, Hager, and Warn 2002)" (Louis 2015, 6). "Studies have shown that school faculties which participate in learning communities focusing on concrete instructional practices and collegiality possess high levels of commitment and satisfaction" (Shouppe and Pate 2010, 8).

44 "Teachers who feel appreciated, connected, and energized by their colleagues bring out the best in their students" (May and Sanders 2013, 9). "Reeves (2009) challenged the belief that professional development programs and lectures (outside experts) are sufficient to change professional practice. He believed that many schools ignore research evidence supporting the power of direct modeling by classroom teachers as a key to professional learning. Yost, Vogel, and Rosenberg (2009) examined the results of a teacher leadership-training model (Project Achieve) and suggested that, when teachers are given chances to improve their teaching practice through on-site, personalized, professional development led by other teachers, increased student learning follows" (Parsons and Beauchamp 2012, 6–7).

45 "The principal invests teachers with resources and instructional support (Rosenblum, Louis, and Rossmiller 1994) and maintains congruence and consistency of the educational program (Conley and Goldman 1994)" (Marks and Printy 2003, 5). "According to the document's preamble, 'The principal is an accomplished teacher who practices quality leadership in the provision of opportunities for optimum learning and development of all students in the school' (Alberta Education 2009)" (Parsons and Beauchamp 2012, 2).

46 "In an article critiquing top-down directives for school improvement, Gallinger (2009) introduced the concept of 'kairos' to describe 'appro-

priateness for the occasion at hand' and argued that educational pol-
icymaking, teaching, and assessment are most effective and ethical
when carried out at the local level" (Parsons and Beauchamp 2012, 7).

[47] "The principal's biggest strength is utilizing all their resources in a
comprehensive way with the ultimate goal of student achievement"
(Brown, 2016, 6).

[48] "A top-down approach in leadership could inhibit organizational
learning by preventing flexibility or teacher division in meeting the
needs of diverse learners." (Rautiola 2009, 6)

[49] "The final component of the PLE theory is that the learning environment is community centered—that is, it focuses on the social nature
of learning, including the norms and modes of operation of any community" (Brown 2016, 3). "Engaging communities. Conceptualized
and included only in Leithwood's model of TSL, leaders demonstrate
sensitivity to community aspirations and requests, incorporate community characteristics and clues in the school, and actively encourage
parents and guardians to become involved in their children's education" (Sun and Leithwood 2012, 12).

[50] "Personalization (in Phase 4) was reflected in an increasing emphasis on teaching that promoted more participative, interdependent,
independent, and flexible learning and that supported a range of
approaches to pupil learning" (Day, Gu, and Sammons 2016, 23).
"Studies have shown that school faculties which participate in learning
communities focusing on concrete instructional practices and collegiality possess high levels of commitment and satisfaction [and] [l]ead-
ership focused on the development of teachers' knowledge and skills,
professional community and school climate could lead to improved
student academic performance" (Shouppe and Pate 2010, 8).

[51] "These models implemented leadership team methods such as including teachers, principals and parents to play key roles in the organizational structure, curriculum and instruction" (Rautiola 2009, 10).

[52] The inefficiency of using standardized testing to measure school effectiveness dates back, at least, to 1978 (Lock and Lummis 2014, 63).
In addition, experts have called for "utilization of multiple forms of
assessments to determine school effectiveness" (Green 2010, 5).

[53] "Although it is acknowledged that measurable outcomes of students'
academic progress and achievement are key indicators in identify-

ing school "effectiveness," they are insufficient to define "successful" schools. A range of leadership research conducted in many contexts over the past two decades shows clearly that "successful" schools strive to educate their pupils by promoting positive values (integrity, compassion, fairness, and love of lifelong learning), as well as fostering citizenship and personal, economic, and social capabilities (Day and Leithwood 2007; Ishimaru 2013; Mulford and Silins 2011; Putnam 2002)" (Day, Gu, and Sammons 2016, 3).

[54] The collective benefits of the PLC structure can be found by examining Parsons and Beauchamp (2012), Gautam, Alford, and Khanal (2015), Shouppe and Pate (2010), Masumoto and Brown-Welty (2009), Lashway (2003).

[55] "The principal should give the same weight to ideas from all members of the school community (faculty, staff, students, and parents) when designing a plan to achieve the school's goals" (Gantner, Newsom, and Dunlap 2000, 13). "Improving outcomes requires a team of teachers, students, parents, and community members, all working in collaboration" (Hattie 2015, 4). "Trust includes a belief or expectation on the part of most teachers that their colleagues, students, and parents support the schools' goals for student learning and will reliably work toward achieving those goals" (Leithwood, Patten, and Jantzi 2010, 7). "The role of principal has since evolved into one in which the principal must understand the needs of their students, staff, community and the curriculum" (Luu 2010, 1).

[56] "[NASE principals] strive to create a 'we are all in this together' attitude and organization…They strive to provide all in their school community with a sense of ownership in the school and collective belief in its mission" (National Association for Schools of Excellence (NASE) and Northwest Regional Educational Laboratory (NWREL) 1999, 16).

[57] "In addition, these teachers emphasized their role in addressing students' social and academic needs such as the need to improve students' self-esteem, to increase student responsibility, and to teach lifelong learning, 'encourage students to challenge themselves…develop a sense of excitement about their education'(144)" (Mendez-Morales 1992, 35).

[58] "Marshall and Oliva (2006, 196) declared that education leaders, 'must be able to present arguments that educational excellence means moving beyond test scores and working with parents and communities to build inclusive, safe, and trusting spaces'" (Hughes and Jones 2010, 59).

[59] "By developing a school culture that fosters student success and building leadership models, which include teachers, principals, parents to play key roles in the organizational structure, curriculum and instruction, can increase the potential to indirectly lead to increased student achievement" (Rautiola 2009, 23). "Leadership focused on the development of teachers' knowledge and skills, professional community and school climate could lead to improved student academic performance" (Shouppe and Pate 2010, 8).

[60] "Increasingly, practicing principals find themselves engaged in the management of public

[61] "[Parents and teachers] learned from [principal] how to communicate more openly about student learning, and how to become more active learners themselves [. . .] [Principal] restructured the school to facilitate learning through teamwork, collaborative planning, and shared decision making, which distributed leadership to teachers so they could better understand and address their own professional learning needs" (Jacobson, Brooks, Giles, Johnson, and Ylimaki 2007, 18). "The best situation is one of cohesion; where this is impossible the recruitment of a majority of the parents and community is basic. When schools fail in their basic task of instruction, the parents pick up the burden and bear the brunt. In one study school, the data seem to indicate that whatever learning occurred there during the study year was more the result of parental and home influence than school effects [. . .]. The highest achieving school for the study year treated parents as equals in a partnership" (Sizemore 1983, 20).

[62] "In terms of creating productive community relationships, principals made efforts to 'provide parents with the opportunity to participate in school management through parent committees', and were 'effective in building community support for the school's improvement efforts'" (Liu 2013, 19).

[63] Instead of schools having to solicit parental participation, the PLC culture increases parent-initiated supports, as they feel empowered by their sense of ownership within the process (Edmonds 1979).

64 "[School leaders] must rally students, teachers, parents, local health and family service agencies, youth development groups, local businesses and other community residents and partners around the common goal of raising student performance. And they must have the leadership skills and knowledge to exercise the autonomy and authority to pursue these strategies" (Lashway 2003, 3).

65 "Partnerships with parents, business professionals, and organizations were established to address college, career, and technical needs of students and families [. . .]. Resources were strategically utilized to overcome drawbacks of poverty, rural circumstances, and non-English speaking communities" (Masumoto and Brown-Welty 2009, 10). "In recent years, a shift has occurred in the locus of some decision making from school districts to the school site level. In some cases this has been in response to perceived wisdom in locating decision making closest to the point of implementation, a trend that is shared in a number of public policy domains and in the political rhetoric" (Portin 1997, 8).

66 "Nationwide, school officials have criticized PPPs for not ensuring that graduates are 'ready' for principalship. They often claim that students graduating from college and university PPPs lack the skills to step right in as effective leaders; instead, they need too much on-the-job learning" (Dodson 2014, 42). "Principals have found themselves lacking adequate knowledge to address the challenges of facilitating administrative and school visions; assuring that students are learning; relating to faculty, staff, and community in a cooperative environment; and implementing new strategies to accomplish change" (Gantner, Newsom, and Dunlap 2000, 5). "For principals who lacked the skills to accomplish [instructional leadership tasks], coaching and on-site assistance were in short supply" (Marks and Printy 2003, 372).

67 "A recent publication sponsored by Division A of the American Educational Research Association (the largest association of its kind in the world, with many international members) claimed that research on school leadership has generated few robust claims. The main reasons cited for this gap in our knowledge was a lack of programmatic research, a paucity of accumulated evidence from both small- and large-scale studies, the use of a variety of research designs, and failure to provide evidence in sufficient amounts and of sufficient quality to

serve as powerful guides to policy and practice" (Leithwood, Harris, and Hopkins 2008, 11).

68 The debate between instructional, transformational, and hybrid leadership has stagnated focused training and preparation of school leaders (Liu 2013; Robinson, Lloyd, and Rowe 2008).

69 "In his criticism, Burns claims that leadership is nowadays universally mediocre, and at times, simply irresponsible. Much of this is to do with our ignorance of the meaning of leadership in modernity. In essence, we are not sure of what leadership is" (Young 2002, 1). "There is no magic bullet; research can give us promising lines of thinking but never a complete answer. To some extent, each group must build its own model and develop local ownership through its own process" (Fullan 2000, 2). "The role of the principal as instructional leader is too narrow a concept to carry the weight of the kinds of reforms that will create the schools that we need for the future" (Fullan 2002, 1).

70 "The importance of the role of the principal as change agent and instructional leader consistently appears in the research on change and effective schools" (Leech and Fulton 2008, 5). "In a school setting, the leadership behaviors the principal employs can be the difference between achieving high levels of academic success or failure" (Siegrist et al. 2009, 2).

71 "While everyone supports the idea that education is a team effort, it is imperative that the team be led by a strong and dedicated leader" (National Association for Schools of Excellence (NASE) and Northwest Regional Educational Laboratory (NWREL) 1999, 8).

72 "This claim emerges from recent research initiatives, and we believe that its implications for leadership have not yet been fully grasped. The basic assumptions underlying the claim are that (a) the central task for leadership is to help improve employee performance; and (b) such performance is a function of employees' beliefs, values, motivations, skills and knowledge and the conditions in which they work. Successful school leadership, therefore, will include practices helpful in addressing each of these inner and observable dimensions of performance—particularly in relation to teachers, whose performance is central to what pupils learn" (Leithwood, Harris, and Hopkins 2008, 4).

73 "A schoolwide culture of learning includes an emphasis on adult learning as well as student learning with both administrators and teachers

engaging in learning activities in a process of ongoing growth and development" (Gautam, Alford, and Khanal 2015, 3). "Improving outcomes requires a team of teachers, students, parents, and community members, all working in collaboration" (Hattie 2015, 4). "The central tenets of PLCs include the following: collaborative cultures, the dismantling of teacher isolation, and highly effective teams that focus on learning" (Reed and Swaminathan 2014, 6).

[74] "Teachers depended on the principal for continued interest and support" (Printy, Marks, and Bowers 2009, 14). "But when schools start to become less stable, and take on the characteristics of a 'frontier culture,' strong formal leadership is typically sought by members of the community in order to reestablish coherence and direction" (Jacobson et al. 2007, 3).

[75] "Research has determined that effective leadership requires both transactional and transformational elements" (Hallinger 2003, 10). "The absence of shared instructional leadership in schools that lacked transformational leadership is an important finding. Whereas transformational leadership is its prerequisite, moreover, shared instructional leadership will not develop unless it is intentionally sought and fostered. This latter finding supports the observation of Hallinger and Leithwood (1998) that transformational leadership does not imply instructional leadership" (Marks and Printy 2003, 23).

[76] Northouse (2013, 185–215) details the progression of the development of the transformational leadership concept.

[77] Supportive research includes: Liu (2013), May and Sanders (2013), Nash (2011), Quin, Debris, Bischoff, and Johnson (2015), Ross and Gray (2006), and Sun and Leithwood (2012); see references for full citations.

[78] "Transformational leadership originated in studies of political leaders. The model focuses on the leader's role in fostering a collective vision and motivating members of an organization to achieve extraordinary performance (Bass 1985)" (Hallinger 2003, 2).

[79] "Although the importance transformational leadership places on vision building can create a fundamental and enduring sense of purpose in the organization, the model lacks an explicit focus on teaching and learning" (Marks and Printy 2003, 377).

80 Instructional leadership was shown to have three to four times' greater impact on student achievement than transformational leadership. However, transformational leadership is shown to have small indirect influence on student achievement or social student outcomes and consistently predicted the willingness of teachers and educational staff to exert extra effort and change past practice or attitudes (Rautiola 2009, 23).

81 "Cookbook approaches to training packages that limit opportunities for principals to adapt research findings to their settings are, therefore, likely to be counterproductive (Barth 1990; Hallinger 1992; Marsh 1992)" (Hallinger, Bickman, and Davis 1996, 18). "Urban school leaders are often seeking the most innovative, best practices to make quick improvements and avoid sanctions" (Reed and Swaminathan 2014, 2).

82 "Although they report ruts concerning principal leadership, the effective schools studies conducted during the 1970s and 1980s were not designed as investigations of leadership. Thus, they often yielded ambiguous findings concerning the nature of the principal's leadership role in school improvement (Hallinger and Murphy 1985; Leithwood et al. 1990; Rowan et al. 1982)" (Hallinger, Bickman, and Davis 1996, 3).

83 Many of the interrelational traits demonstrated by the observed principals were omitted from many findings (Edmonds 1979; Mendez-Morse 1992; Sizemore 1983). In addition, the immediate, post-desegregation school setting still operated without the resources, supports, and access their non-minority counterparts received.

84 Niece (1993, 15) identified eight "Instructional Leadership Descriptors Different from the Authorities' Descriptors," all of which can be categorized as either PLC or transformational.

85 "Research has determined that effective leadership requires both transactional and transformational elements" (Hallinger 2003, 10). "Our synthesis of TSL practices is essentially the "integrated" model (transformational plus instructional) advocated by some educational leadership theorists (e.g., Marks and Printy 2003) and an important implication of Robinson et al.'s (2008) comparison of transformational and instructional leadership effects" (Sun and Leithwood 2012, 23).

86 "The principal's transformational approach eased the way with teachers for her more directive instructional behavior" (Printy, Marks, and Bowers 2009, 13).

87 "The most commonly researched leadership models that have been identified as resulting in success are 'instructional' and 'transformational'" (Day, Gu, and Sammons 2016, 4). "Moreover, the available evidence suggests that transformational leadership is no easier to exercise than instructional leadership" (Hallinger 2013, 14).

88 "The absence of shared instructional leadership in schools that lacked transformational leadership is an important finding. Whereas transformational leadership is its prerequisite, moreover, shared instructional leadership will not develop unless it is intentionally sought and fostered. This latter finding supports the observation of Hallinger and Leithwood (1998) that transformational leadership does not imply instructional leadership" (Marks and Printy, 23).

89 "Based on this line of thought, we suggest that future efforts to conceptualize leadership reflect the practices that seem important across most organizational sectors (primarily transformational leadership practices) as well as practices that are uniquely designed to improve the 'technical core' of the organization. In schools, the technical core is instruction, and this has led us to propose a series of practices included in a dimension we call 'improving instruction' (Leithwood and Jantzi 2005; Leithwood et al. 2004; Leithwood and Riehl 2005)" (Leithwood and Sun 2012, 24).

90 "Moving away from hierarchical notions of leadership, Louis, Kruse and Marks (1996) talk of principals being 'at the center' of the school, rather than 'at the top'" (Christie and Lingard 2001, 18). "Shared leadership is presented as a new style of leadership based on collaboration and consensus building. One in which the principal will, 'Orchestrate a governing process, rather than provide solitary decision making' (Aieta, Barth, and O'Brien 1988, 18)" (Portin 1997, 5).

91 Printy, Marks, and Bowers (2009, 505–506) examined the reasoning behind the need of transformational practices as prerequisites for shared leadership. The study further discovered that the transformational practices were not limited to the administration but, for the high-performing schools, also were demonstrated by the teachers.

93

Either way, the presence of transformational practices is essential for establishing the shared leadership culture.

[92] "The role of the principal as instructional leader is too narrow a concept to carry the weight of the kinds of reforms that will create the schools that we need for the future" (Fullan 2000, 1). "Halpin (1966) stated that one of the major findings resulting from the LBDQ data was that 'effective leadership behavior tends most often to be associated with high performance on both [. . .] the tasks and human aspects of their organizations (97)'" (Mendez-Morse, 1992,14).

[93] The instructional and human motivational tasks of leadership are largely stressed, however, as part of both is the need for the foundational belief that the students can learn (Edmonds 1979; Sizemore 1983).

[94] "Finally, leadership succession research indicates that unplanned headteacher succession is one of the most common sources of schools' failure to progress, in spite of what teachers might do"; "One explanation for this is that leadership serves as a catalyst for unleashing the potential capacities that already exist in the organization" (Leithwood, Harris, and Hopkins 2008, 4).

[95] "This new label denoting a shift to leadership is supposed to be suggestive of a political empowering of principals (Gunter 2004, 21), but in actual practice they remain bound by the centralized directives through policies, guidelines, accountability measures, and public expectations" (Heystek 2007, 4). "To create lasting change, there must be a change in governance through a redistribution of power and control" (Leech and Fulton, 5).

[96] "Clearly, for policy makers, greater attention needs to be directed toward assessing the impact of policy decision on practitioners in the field. When a new policy is proposed, the impact of layered responsibility should be considered more fully in the planning process" (Portin 1997, 17).

[97] "Mortimore and Sammons (1991, 4) asserted that 'the variation between [successful and less successful] schools can be accounted for by differences in school policies within the control of the principal and teachers'" (Leech and Fulton 2008, 5). "Historically and commonly, the decision-making in school systems has been and continues to be hierarchical. Boards of Education set policy and superintendents

determine programs and directives. Lower administrative echelons are informed and held accountable for implementation" (Sizemore 1983, 8).

98 "Given the importance of transformational leadership as a contributing factor to school climate, it would be reasonable to conclude that regular evaluation of a principal's leadership characteristics should be conducted"; "The MLQ-5X could be administered to potential hires as a means of determining the transformational leadership characteristics that person will exhibit" (Allen, Grigsby, and Peters 2015, 18).

99 "Added to the traditional duties of managing personnel, transportation, campus maintenance, discipline, and curriculum, today's principals are 'increasingly responsible for shared decision making, decentralized budgeting, collaborative planning, and increased accountability' (Peterson 2001, 18)"; "School systems and school boards should examine their hiring and retention practices for principals in an effort to increase their longevity in the position" (Siegrist et al. 2009, 1–4).

100 "In spite of compelling research supporting a positive school climate as a fundamental component in school effectiveness and student achievement, policymakers have been reluctant to recognize climate as a measurable leading indicator and a precursor to future success"; "Cohen et al. (2009, 196) point to a 'growing awareness that we need to not only consider the measurement of cognitive gains, but also the social, emotional, and ethical dimensions of school life'" (May and Sanders 2013, 10).

101 "Nationwide, school officials have criticized PPPs for not ensuring that graduates are "ready" for principalship. They often claim that students graduating from college and university PPPs lack the skills to step right in as effective leaders; instead, they need too much on-the-job learning" (Dodson 2014, 42).

102 "Principals have found themselves lacking adequate knowledge to address the challenges of facilitating administrative and school visions; assuring that students are learning; relating to faculty, staff, and community in a cooperative environment; and implementing new strategies to accomplish change" (Gantner, Newsom, and Dunlap 2000, 5).

103 "It is recommended that principal preparation programs incorporate Kouzes and Posner's transformational leadership model into their cur-

riculum in order to develop highly qualified school leaders" (Quin et al. 2015, 1).

[104] "The first meta-analysis indicated that the average effect of instructional leadership on student outcomes was three to four times that of transformational leadership" (Robinson, Lloyd, and Rowe 2008, 635).

[105] "Research has determined that effective leadership requires both transactional and transformational elements" (Hallinger 2003, 10). "This has given rise to recent descriptions of school leadership that combine practices associated with both transformational and instructional leadership models (Leithwood, Louis, Anderson, and Wahlstrom 2004; H. M. Marks and Printy 2003; Robinson, Hohepa, and Lloyd 2009)" (Leithwood and Sun 2012, 3). "Instructional, distributed, and transformational leadership practices at school and district levels were important elements contributing to changes in classroom instruction and increased student achievement" (Masumoto and Brown-Welty 2009, 9).

[106] Leech, D., and Fulton, C. (2008). Faculty perception of shared decision making and the principal's leadership behaviors in secondary schools in a large urban district. *Education*, 128(4), 630–644.

[107] "The same approach to school leadership from the principal will simply not be appropriate across all such contexts" (Hallinger, Bickman, and Davis 1996, 6).

[108] "One implication for practicing leaders is the extension of what it means to make evidence-informed decisions [. . .]. Such decisions would need to include considerations of research evidence about variables with demonstrable effects on student learning and how leaders influence the condition or status of those variables" (Leithwood, Patten, and Jantzi 2010, 27).

[109] "Rather, successful principals draw differentially on elements of both instructional and transformational leadership and tailor (layer) their leadership strategies to their particular school contexts and to the phase of development of the school" (Day, Gu, and Sammons 2016, 33).

[110] "Organizational policy needs to support an understanding and appreciation of the maverick who is willing to take unpopular positions, who knows when to reject the conventional wisdom, and who takes

reasonable risks" (Bass 1990, 8–9). "Any extraordinary method for accelerating the acquisition of leadership skills, attitudes and attributes is yet to be discovered [. . .]. It seems to be the nature of the human being to acquire leadership skills a little at a time—building upon previously learned precepts" (Carraway 1990, 21).

[111] Once the leader has mastered the second step of the process they can then utilize alternate means of practice identification (i.e., professional development, seminars, etc.).